PROCESSIONERS' RECORDS
CHOWAN COUNTY
NORTH CAROLINA

- 1755/1756; 1764/1765; 1795-1797; 1800 and 1808 -

Compiled by:
Raymond Parker Fouts

Southern Historical Press, Inc.
Greenville, South Carolina

This volume was reproduced
from a personal copy located in
the Publishers private library

Please direct all correspondence and book orders to:

SOUTHERN HISTORICAL PRESS, Inc.
PO Box 1267
Greenville, SC 29602-1267

ISBN #978-1-63914-249-1
Printed in the United States of America

PREFACE

These records have been transcribed verbatim from xerographic and microfilm copies of the originals found in the North Carolina State Archives, Raleigh, North Carolina. [Stack File #C.R.024.408.2, Chowan County Misc. Land Records 1708-1923, Patent-Survey and microfilm reel #C.024.48006, Chowan County Processioners' Record, 1756, 1795-1808.] Their existence was kindly made known to the writer by William Doub Bennett.

The Lords Proprietors enacted "An Act, for settling the Titles and Bounds of Lands." 23 November 1723. This act directed that the Justices of each Precinct Court should order the vestry of each Parish to divide them into convenient districts for processioning every person's land between 1 October and the last day of April, following the order of the Court. This was to be done "in every three years." Two freeholders were to perform the processioning and were required to make a return of their proceedings to the next Court, including any lands which had not been processioned and the reasons for failing. Persons who had their lands processioned twice were deemed the sole owner.[1] As this law had not had the desired effect, it was altered in 1729 to allow the Vestries to appoint processioners without the Court order.[2]

The Procession Docket contains some information on 13 of the 19 cantons laid out by the Vestry of St. Paul's Parish 25 October 1755. The docket is followed by the original processioners' orders and returns, some of which differ from the clerks' transcriptions. All the pertinent vestry orders for 1755/1756 and 1764/1765 are found in Appendix A. Reduced copies of the originals are provided in Appendix B. A map of St. Paul's Parish as of 1755 appears on page 116.

The order for the return of Edward HARE, Jr., and Joseph SPEIGHT, under the header of "[No date]," does not appear in the Vestry Minutes for St. Paul's Parish. As it includes landowners and landmarks in that part of Chowan County that was cut off to Hertford County [now Gates], that processioning was done prior to 1759.

Each original page has been assigned a number, within parentheses. The name and location indexes refer to these assigned numbers. Any original page numbers that appear in the docket, or on the returns, have been enclosed within brackets and are to the right of the assigned number. The references to names and locations in Appendix A are followed by the letter "a." All names are indexed, including those crossed-out but still legible. Female given names are indexed, in addition to their surname listing.

All surnames have been capitalized, with "hAINS" denoting lower case was used for the initial letter of the surname in the original. The crossed "p" has been typed as "pr." Underlining ["Dority"] denotes emphasis on verbatim spelling. The following letters and words in the various hands are look-alikes: a=o; H=w; J=T; j=z; U=N; u=v; Elijah=Elizah. "/th/" denotes interlined letters or words. "/th/" denotes both interlined and underlined.

[1]Clark, Walter, ed. The State Records of North Carolina, Vol. XXIII, Laws 1715-1776, pp. 103-106. Goldsboro, NC: State of North Carolina, 1904.
[2]Ibid., pp. 114, 115.

TABLE OF CONTENTS

PROCESSIONERS' RECORDS

CHOWAN COUNTY, NORTH CAROLINA

1755/1756; 1764/1765; 1795-1797; 1800 and 1808

PROCESSION DOCKET 1756

(1) [__] Processioned the Line between John KITTEREL and William WATERS both part___ present likewise Daniel PUGH and Richard BAKER.

Processioned the Line between Richard BAKER and John KITTEREL both parties present likewise Daniel PUGH and Stephen PARKER.

Processioned the Line between William WATERS and Richard BAKER both parties present likewise Daniel PUGH and Thomas BAKER.

Processioned the Line between William WATERS and Richard PARKER both Parties present, likewise Daniel PUGH and Jacob BOYCES.

Processioned the Line between Richard BAKER and Richard PARKER both parties present likewise Daniel PUGH and Thomas WIGGINS.

Processioned the Line between Epaphaditus BOYCE and Richard BAKER both parties present likewise Daniel pUGH and Thomas WIGGONS

Processioned the Line between Richard pARKER and Epaphaditus BOYCE both parties present likewise Daniel PUGH and Thomas WIGGONS

Processioned the Line between Daniel pUGH and Epaphaditus BOYCE both parties present likewise Richard BAKER and Thomas WIGGONS

Processioned the Line between Daniel PUGH and Richard BROTHERS both Parties present Thomas WIGGONS & Micajah REDDICK

Processioned the Line between Daniel PUGH and Elizabeth ALLEN both Parties present, likewise Thomas WIGGONS and Stephen PARKER

Processioned the Line between Daniel PUGH and William WATERS both Parties present, likewise Thomas WIGGONS and Stephen PARKER

Processioned the Line between Daniel pUGH and William WATERS both Parties to these presents, likewise Thomas WIGGONS and Andrew MATTHEWS

Processioned the Line between Daniel pUGH and Thomas WIGGONS both Parties present likewise William WATERS and Andrew MATTHEWS.

Processioned the Line between Daniel pUGH and William HUGHS, William HUGHS refuses or neglecting present Moses BENTON George WILLIAMS and Jessie WILLIAMS.

(1) (Cont.) Processioned the Line between John BENTON and Moses PARKER, John BENTON Present.

(2) [__] Processioned the Line between John BENTON and Caleb PELSON present James PARKER and Elijah BENTON.

Processioned the Line between the King and James PARKER present Elijah BENTON and Caleb POLSON.

Processioned the Line between John WILLIAMSON and James PARKER both present, Elijah BENTON Caleb POLSON.

Processioned the Line between King and John WILLIAMSON, John WILLIAMSON Present, James PARKER present.

Processioned the Line between James PARKER and Elijah BENTON, both parties present.

Processioned the Line between Darthy SMITH and William T?RUEWATHAN Both present likewise Amos SMITH.

Processioned the Line between Dority SMITH and Samuel POWELL Both present likewise peter pARKER.

Processioned the Line between Darthy SMITH and Henry MORGAN both present likewise peter pARKER

Processioned the Line between Henry MORGAN and Samuel POWELL both Parties present, likewise peter PARKER.

Processioned the Line between Samuel pOWELL and William TRUEWATHAN both present, likewise Peter PARKER.

Processioned e-A Line for William TRUEWATHAN present Peter PARKER and Henry MORGAN.

Porcessioned a Line between Ephroditus BOYS & William WATERS present both parties likewise Daniel PARKER John HARRIS

Porcessioned the Line between John KITTREL and William HUGGS John KITTREL Present, William HUGGS neglecting or Refusing present George KITTREL Jesse WILLIAMS.

Porssoned (sic) the line betwean John KITTREL Jane WILLIAMS both Parties present likewise George KITTREL

Processoned the Line between William HUGGS & Jane WILLIAMS both parties Present

Porcessoned the Line between William HUGGS and Mary VANN both present

(3) [__] Porcessioned the Lines of William HUGHES all but one Ma__ [Corner of page is folded over.] after they were forwarned by John KITTERELL.

Porcessioned the Lines of John VANNN himself present____

Porcessioned all the Lines Mary VANN she present.____

Porcessioned the Line between Mary SOWARD & George WILLIAMS both present Likewise

(3) (Cont.) Joseph FIGG.

Porcessioned the Lines between George WILLIAMS and the King George WILLIAMS and Joseph FIGG.

Porcessioned the line between Mary SOWARD & the King--George WILLIAMS present.

Porcessioned the line between Mary SOWARD & Lawrance BAKER both present Likewise George WILLIAMS.

Porcessioned the Line between Lawrence BAKER and the King Lawrance BAKER present Likewise William DANIEL

Porcessioned the Lines of John LEWIS Edward VANN present

Porcessioned the Line Between Abraham LACITOR And myLord present the parties John BRINKLEY & Elizah BENTON

Porcessioned the Lines Between Elizah BENTON and abraham LACITOR present both parties Elizah BIRD & John WEB?B Likewise.

Porcessioned the Line Between Elizah BENTON & Lemuel POWELL present Elizah BENTON.
William POWELL}
Richard FELTON} Returns

(4) [6] According to the Order of Vestry We have processioned all the Lands that is within our Bounds, Processioned by us
Jacob ODOM
Jeames BRADEY

ffeb/ry/. 7/th/ 1756. Edward WARREN his Land dun (sic), Demsey BUCKES his Land dun, present Edward VANN and Joseph WAREN

Edward VANN his Land dun James BRADEY his Land dun present Jacob BUCKS Edward VANN & James BRADEY

ffeb. 9/th/ 1756. Jacob BUCKS his Land dun present Demsey BUCKS and Jacob BUCKS James BRADEY and Jacob ODOM.

ffeb/ry/. 10th 1756. James ELLIS seaner (sic) his Land dun James ELLIS Junr. his Land dun James BAKER his Land dun, Samuel BAKER his Land dun, present James ELLIS James BAKER Richard BAKER and John ODOM.

feb/ry/. 10/th/ 1756. William GONES Land dun, John ODOM his Land dun.

Jeathro HARREL his Land dun, present John ODOM and William Roberd KNIGHT James ELLIS Jethro HARREL

feby 11/th/. John pARKER his Land dun, John pARKER his other Land dun present John pARKER John ODOM James ELLIS

Roberd ROGERS his Land dun

ffeb/ry/. 14 1756 Henry GOODMANs his Land dun Joel GOODMAN his Land dun James BRADY his Land dun Edward WARREN his Land dun Isaac pIPKEN his Land dun, William GOODMAN present Henry Robert ROGERS Joel GOODMAN Edward WARREN Isaac pIPKEN William GOODMAN

(4) (Cont.) ffebry. 14/th/ 1756 William SMITH his Land dun, ffrancis BRINKLEY his Land dun, present ffrances BRINKLEY, Robard TOMES William SMITH James TOMES, William FELTON his Land dun.

Robert KNIGHT his Land dun James ELLIS Junr. his Land dun, Thomas LANGSTONE Land un (sic), ffrancis LANGSTONE Land dun, present Robert KNIGHT William FELTEN, Thomas LANGSTON.

ffeb/ry/. 27/th/. 1756 John ODOM his Land dun present Edward WARREN

(5) [7] Febry 27 1756 Edward HARE his Land dun, John LEWIS his Land dun, Joseph BRADLEY his Land dun, John DUKINS his Land dun, Elizebeth HARTLOCK hur Land dun, present Edward HARE, John LEWIS, Joseph BRADEY, John DUCKINS, Elizabeth HARTLOCK.

Febry 28/th/ 1756 Robert ROGERS his Land dun, Stephen ROGERS his Land dun, Thomas LANGSTONE his Land dun, present Robert ROGERS, Stephen ROGERS, Thomas LANGSTONE

Febry 28 1756 John PARKER his Land dun, William U?MFLEET his Land dun present John PARKER William UMFLEET

Febry 28 1756 Thomas HARRELEs his Land dun James BRADAYs his Land dun & William GOODMANs Lands dun, Alexander CARTER his Land dun present Stephen ROGERS Elexander CARTER.

March the 2/d/. 1756 Thomas ODOM his Land dun, Thomas HARELEs his Land dun, Ephrititus GONES his Land dun, Jethro HARREL his Land dun, James ELLIS his Land dun, John ODOMs Swamp dun, present Ephrititus GONES, Jethro HARREL John ODOM Joseph TOMIS

March 11/th/. 1756 Willis REDDICK his Land dun, Stephen SHEPARD two tracts dun, Jacob ODAM his Land dun, Edward VANN his Land dun, present Willis REDDICK, Stephen SHEPARD Joseph NOFLET (sic), Daniel LASITER

March the 16 1756. James TOMIS his Land dun ffrancis BRINKLEY his Land dun, Present Robert TOMIS and James TOMIS and Francis BRINKLEY

Thomas PILAND his Land dun, Edward pILAND his Land dun, Joseph NOFLET present Thomas PILAND Edward PILAND James PILAND Joseph NOFLET

(6) [8] March 26/th/ 1756 Jacob VANN his Land dun, present George VAN (sic) Jacob ROGERS Jacob VANN Elizabeth VANN

March 29th 1756 Henry BACKER his Land dun, at his Mill Joynding (sic) to NOFLET present Joseph NOFLET Henery BAKER, James Bray BAKER, [End of entry.]

ffebry the 21/st/. 1756 Edward HARE Junr. his Land dun, philip PIPKINS his Land dun Moses ODOM his Land dun, present Edward HARE Isaac pIPKINS Moses ODOM.

ffebry the 25. 1756 Edward HARE his Land dun, Edward HARE his Land dun (sic), Isaac WILLIAMS his Land dun, present Edward HARE, Isaac WILLIAMS, Steward PIPKINS his Land dun, Robard pARKER his Land dun present Stuard pIPKIN, Stephen SHEPARD and Robert PARKER, [End of entry.]

March 29/th/ 1756 Edward HAREs his other Land dun James CONNER his Land dun present Edward HARE, James CONNER.

(6) (Cont.) March 27/th/. 1756 Jacob ODOM his Land dun, Joseph KNOWFLEETs (sic) his Land dun, James EUREE his Land dun, present Joseph KNOWFLEET Thomas LANGSTONE, Thomas PILAND his land, William ffRIER his Land dun, [End of entry.]

March 26/th/ 1756 Robert KNIGHT and William JONES there (sic) Land dun, present George VAN

Jacob ODOM, Robert KNIGHT, John PORTER his Land dun

(7) [9] North Carolina}
Chowan County } Persuant to an Order of Vestry bearing date the 25th. Day of October last, for the Processioning of Lands Wehave (sic) agreeable thereto Processioned James HINTONs, William HAYSE, David FULKS, John WALTONs, Gabriel LACETERs, Jeshom LACITERs, Maxemelion MINSHEEs, Richard MINSHEEs Aaron BLANSHARDs, Micajah BLANSHARDs, Timothy WALTONs, William WALTON Sen, William WALTON Junr. James COSTENs, Thomas HOLTs, Richard BONDs, John LACETER's, James BROWNs, Joseph MEASELs and Aaron MEASEL's Lands

Robert LACETER
Moses LACETER

InComplyance (sic) to an Order of Vestry dated the 25/th/. of October 1755 We the Subscribers have precessiened all the Bounds of Land according to order peaceable exsept aline (sic) between Beniamme (sic) BLANCHARD and John WATSON Stopt by thesaid (sic) BLANCHARD

frances SAUNDERS
John MINERY

January the 10/th/. 1756
Processiened parsuant to order, by Abner EASON and Guy HILL Lines
Between Thomas WALTON and Nathaniel SPIVEY
Between Nathaniel SPIVEY and Jacob SPIVEY
Between Jacob SPIVEY and Aron HILL Junr.
Between Jacob SPIVEY and Aron HILL Senr.
Between Timothy WALTEN and Aron HILL Senr
Between Macaiath (sic) BLANCHARD & Aron HILL Senr.
Between Aron HILL Senr. and Aron HILL Junr.

(8) [10] Between Jacob SPIVEY and Ephraim BLANCHARD
Between Ephraim BLANCHARD and Benjamin BLANCHARD
Between Macajah BLANCHARD and Benjamin BLANCHARD
Between Amous BLANCHARD and Aron BLANCHARD
Between James GRIFFIN and Joseph GRIFFIN.
Between James GRIFFEN and Abraham HILL
Between James GRIFFEN and Guy HILL.
Between Guy HILL and ~~James~~? [overwritten] Jonas SPIVEY
Between Jonas SPIVEY and James GRIFFEN
Between Jonas SPIVEY and Joal SPIVEY
Between Jaal SPIVEY and Moses ROUNTREE
Between Joal SPIVEY and Abraham HILL
Between Joal SPIVEY and Edward BERRYMAN
Between George EASON and Benjamin BEREYMAN
Between Samuel STALLINGS and James SCOT
Between George EASON and James SCOT
Between James SCOT and Beniamin BEREYMAN
Between George EASON and Benjamin BEREYMAN,
Between George EASON and Abner EASON,
Between Abner EASON and Edward BEREYMAN,
Between Abner EASON and Guy HILL, ~~BERRYMAN~~

(8) (Cont.) Between Guy HILL and Abraham HILL,
Between Abraham HILL and Edward BEREYMAN
Between Guy HILL and Moses ROUNDTREE
Between John EVENS and Joseph GRIFFEN
Between Joseph GRIFFEN and William WALTON,
Between William WALTON and Edward TROTMON
Between Edward TROTMON and Moses ROUNTREE
Between Jacob DOCTON and Moses PEARCE
Between Luke SUMNER and Joal HUNTER,
Between Elisha HUNTER and William HUNTER,

(9) [11] Between Elisha HUNTER and Samuel GREEN
Between Samuel GREEN and William EASON,
Between William EASON and Joseph HURDLEE
Between Joseph HURDLEE and Jacob DOCTON
Between Jacob SPIEGHT and George EASON Senr.

Persuant to an Order of Vestry dated the 15/th/ of October 1755 We the Subscribers have processiened all the Lands within the Destrict mentioned in the said Order as by above List dated the 6th of April 1756 pr Abner EASON
Guy HILL

NorthCarolinaChowanCount (sic) April the 5th. 1756
Persuant to an Order of Vestry past the 25th. of October 1755 We the Subscribers being appointed processioners to procession a Canton laid out for them by the said Vestry Beginning at BENNETs Creek Bridge so along BENNETs Creek Road to Cathrin Creek Bridge so down the said Creek to the River thence up the River to BENNETs Creek thence up the said Creek to the afd. Bridge And accordingly We met and Qualifyed And then processiened all the Lands within the said Canton, Only Mr. James WILSON and Henry HILL refuses to Procession with Jesse HUNTER and Edward PEYLAND refuses to procession with James WILSON
Benjamin BLANSHARD
Jesse HUNTER

(10) [12] In Persuance to an Order of Vestry bearing Date the 15th. of December 1755 We processioned all the Lands in our Bounds as follows.
Processioned the Line between James WILSON and George PILAND Both Parties present

Processioned the Line between George PILAND and John ALSTON both Parties present

Processioned the Line between George PILAND and Henry BAKER both Parties Present

Processioned the Line between Henry BAKER and John ALSTON both parties present

Processioned the Line between Henry BAKER and William HAYS both Parties present

Processioned the Lines between Henry BAKER and William HAYS both Parties present (sic)

Processioned the Lines between John ALSTON and James BROWN Senr both Parties present

Processioned the Line between John ALSTON and William HAYS Senr. both parties present

Processioned the Line between John ALSTON and Barsheba SUMNER both parties present

Processioned the Line between Thomas SUMNER and John ALSTON both parties present

(10) (Cont.) Processioned the Line between William DANIEL and William REDDICK both parties present

Processioned the Line between William REDDICK and Joh (sic) MADDERY both parties present

Processioned the Line between William RIDDICK and Laurence BAKER both parties present

(11) [13] Processioned the Line between Henry BAKER and John MADARIE? both parties present

Processioned the Line between Laurence BAKER and Mary SOWARD both Parties Present.

Processioned the Line between George PILAND and Jeames PILAND both Parties Present

Wm DANIEL
James PILAND

Persuant to an order of Vestry dated October 15/th/. 1756 We the Subscribers have processioned all the Lands Marks within the district in the said Order mentioned as follows vizt

Between Whome	Persons Present
William POWELL and George GORDON	the same
Marmaduke NORFLET & George GORDON	thesame (sic)
Ditto and Isaac HILL.	the Same
Lemuel POWEL and Ditto	Isaac HILL
Elizabeth NORFLET & Lemuel POWELL	David JONES
Ditto-and David JONES	Ditto . . .
Ditto and Moses HAIR	Ditto
Thomas PARKER & Ditto	Ditto
Peter BRINKLEY and David JONES .	Ditto
George GORDON & Ditto	Ditto and Peter BRINKLEY
Ditto and Francis POWELL	Ditto
James JONES and Ditto	Ditto Jethro PEELE
Demsey JONES and Thomas WIGGENS	Jethro BENTON and ==== Jesse PEELE
====Jesse PEELE and Daniel PUGH .	Ditto
Ditto and Jethro BENTON	Ditto
Jethro BENTON and Marmaduke NORFLET--	Ditto and Daniel BENTON
Daniel PUGH and Ditto	Ditto & Ditto
Epaproditus BENTON & Jethro BENTON	Ditto and Ditto
James PARKER and Ditto	Ditto and Ditto
Joseph JONES and William PARKER--	Thomas PARKER

(12) [14]

Between Whome	Persons Present
William PARKER and Eliz/a/. NORFLET --	Thomas PARKER
Thomas PARKER and Wm. PARKER --	Joseph JONES
Joseph JONES & Edward ARNELL	William PARKER
Demsey SUMNER & Benj/a/. pARKER	Jethro BENTON
Ditto and James PARKER	Ditto
Thomas HIGGENS and Thomas FRAZER	Benjamin PARKER
Benjamin PARKER & Ditto	Thomas HIGGENS
Thomas HIGGENS & John KNIGHT	Sturges EDERENGAME
John KNIGHT & Edw/d/. ARNELL	Thomas WIGGENS
Luke SUMNER & Saml. SUMNER -	William SUMNER
William SUMNER & Ditto	Sturges EDERENGAME
Edward ARNELL & Thomas WIGGENS --	John KNIGHT

(12) (Cont.) April 2/d/. 1756
William POWELL
Edward ARNELL

February 4/th/. 1756
Then Processioned all the Lands of William FREEMAN Joseph TAYLOR Richard FREEMAN Ralph OUTLAW Jonathan WALLISS Hanse HOFFLER James SUMNER.

5/th/. Processioned theLands (sic) of Charles ROUNDTREE Thomas WALTON Christen WARD Thomas ROUNDTREE Amos HOBBS William W‡ALLIS John HOBBS Guy HOBBS.

6/th/. Processioned theLands of Thomas HOBBS Mary EASON Lewis OUTLAW.

7/th/. Samuel PERRY's Land David SUMNER George WHITE Stephen THOMAS Joseph DEBLIN.

(13) [15] 15/th/. March processioned the Lands of Richard GARRET Rubin HINTON Richard CHAPILL, Christen WARD, Edward NUGEN, Briget WARD,--

17/th/ Thomas WARD, Lewis WARD, Thomas WARD Jr. Joseph WARD, Christine WARD, Ann WARD.

18/th/ Benjamin WARD, Elexander MACLENY, James WARD, John WARD, Samuel PARKS, Joseph COPLEN, Edward NUGEN, John GOODING Richard GOODING, Joseph GOODIN, James SUMNER, Daniel ROGERS, Joseph WINSLO, John HODSON.

20/th/. Timothy LILLEY, Joseph LILLEY, Leny HOLAWAY, Hardy HURDLE, Richard FELTON, James, EASON, Mary EASON, Diner COPLEN, Richard HARRELL, James SCOTT, Thomas GARRETT, Thomas HOBBS, Barnaby HOBBS

Persuant to and in Obedience of an Order of the Vestry of StPauls (sic) Parish appointing us the Subscribers Processioners to Procession all the Lands Included between Cathrins Creek the Sandy Run and Perquimons Road, and to make a return there of to the County Court &c This may certifye that We have accordingly processioned the Same according to the within List, of the Owners Names Witness our Hands This Sixth day of April 1756
James SUMNER
Richard FREEMAN

An Account oftheLines (sic) Processiened by Luke WHITE and Wm. BOYD and fresh Marked Vizt. Between Richard GARRETT, John BACUR and William BOYD from Indian Creek to Rockahock Swamp then from aGum standing in the Ridge of the said Swamp to aGum in the Horse Pen Pecosin Between Samuel WOODWARD and William BOYD down a Line of Markt Trees between John WALLIS and BOYD

(14) [16] Present Samuel WOODWARD John WALLIS then Between John WALLIS and Samuel WOODWARD to WOODWARDs Corner Tree an Old Poplar new Markt, a Small Oake, WOODWARD and WALLACE present. Apart (sic) of WALLISes disputed by Edward WOODWARD from the aforesaid Corner Tree to the Horse pen Pocosin, then from the poly Bridge Swamp along lines Between William BOYDs and the WOODWARDs Lands and Between the said Lands and Some Land held by William LEWIS then Between the wOODWARDs and miles HALSEY from the DIDY? House Down to the Rich Neck Swamp Edward WOODWARD and Miles HALSEY present then from Rockahock Creek along a line of Marked Trees between Samuel MC. GUIRE and Miles HALSEY they present then /between/ Samuel MC GUIRE and abraham NORFLEET along aLine of Marked Trees down to Rockahock Trees (sic) MC GUIRE and NORFLEET present Then Between Jacob PREVIT and William BOYD they present along aline of Marked Trees then round between the Lands heldby William LEWIS and Jacob PREVITT Frances JAMESs Orphans and Shadrick BUNCH a line of Marked Trees to the Land Entred by Jesse BUNCH Present--Shadrick BUNCH and PREVITT then Between the Entred Land and Shadrick BUNCH a line of Marked Trees

(14) (Cont.) down to the river pocosen then from the River pecosen Between BUNCHes Entry and Thomas HUBBARDs a line of Marked Trees to HARVEYs Corner Tree then along a line HUBBARD (sic) David AMBROSE present, of Marked Trees Bound HUBBARDs and PRIDHAMs Land to Mr. CRAVENs Corner Tree then along aline of Marked Trees to alocus (sic) Tree on the River Near the horse landing then from Rockahock Creek along aline of Marked Trees between James QUIN and Mr. CRAVENs Land to QUINs Corner Tree present Lewis JONES then Between Lewis JONES and QUINs to the Miry Branch Lewis JONES--

(15) [17] present then between Lewis JONES and David AMBROSE from Rockahock Creek to their Corner Tree then round the Rest of AMBROSEs Lines to Rockahock Creek then from the river between Luke WHITE and William BOYD aline of Marked Trees to the Poly Bridge--Swamp then between Luke WHITE and John WALLIS aline of Marked Trees to the Rooty Branch then Between Luke /WHITE/ and John CAMPBELL Esqr. along aline of Marked Trees to the river andno (sic) further pr Wm. BOYD
Luke WHITE

In Persuance to an Order of Vestry Barring (sic) Date the 15/th/. of December 1756 Wehave (sic) processiened all the following Lands in our Bounds as follows--Procesiened yeLines between Elisha HUNTER and John GORDON

Processiened ye Lines between Jacob HUNTER and Samuel HARREL parties pres/t/,

Processiened ye Lines between Av?ron LACITER and William RICE

Processiened the Lines between John RICE and Judah JONES

Processioned the Lines between Samuel HARREL and Mr. BOYD

Processioned the Lines between Aron LACITER and Thomas FULLINGTON

Processioned the Lines between Josiah GRANBERRY and John HARRIS

Processioned the Lines between Robert POWELL and Abraham HILL

Processioned the Lines between John DAVIS and the Widow BRIGS

Processioned the Lines between Abraham HILL and the Widow HINTON.

Processioned the Lines between William RICE and Judah JONES

Processioned the Lines between Rulen [or Ruben] PHELPS and Moses SPIGHT

Processioned the Lines between Daniel PUGH and James WIGINS

Processioned the Lines between James PHELPS and Josu?ah SMALL

Processioned the Lines between Daniel PUGH and Richard BOND
all parties present pr. us John RICE
Samuel HARRELL

(16) [18] Janary the 29/th/. 1756
Processioned for William GOODMAN beginning at aPine afore and aft tree in a ===Runing Line to apine aCorner tree between William GOODMAN and William LANG aRuning Line to apine aCorner Tree aRuning to a Gum aCorner tree aRuning Line to apine aCorne (sic) tree of James LANG present Robert ROGERS and John

(16) (Cont.) WEBB a runing Line between William GOODMAN and Robert ROGERS to apine Corner Tree of Wm. GOODMAN aruning Line tree to the Road present Isaac PIPKIN and Robert ROGERS, Processioned for Isaac PIPKIN aruning Line to the Run of the Bever Dam to a pine aCorner tree of Isaac PIPKINs a runing Line between Wm. GOODMAN and Isaac PIPKIN to the road present William GATTLING Jr. and Jon. WEBB beginning at the Senter three Pines of Thomas BARNS a Runing Line tree to the sente (sic) of three Pines of John WINBORNs Line a Runing Line to aRod Oak aCorner tree of Frances BRINKLEY Line to aWhite Oak a Corner Tree of John ODOM Line a runing Line to apine tree aCorner tree of John ODOMs Present John SKINER and Jacob ODOM aruning Line from a Red Oak to a pine aCorner tree of Thomas BARNS a runing Line between John ODOM and Thomas BARNES to the Senter of three Trees Present Jon SKINNER and Jacob ODOM beginning at aWhite Oak aCorner tree of James THOMAS aRuning Line to a /white/ Oak a corner tree then aruning Line to aWhite Oak to aCorner tree Then a Runing Line to aWhite Oak a Corner tree of John SKINNER then aruning Line to a Branch, Present Jac? ODOM Jon. ODOM and William FELTON Jur. begining at aWater Oak aCorner tree of Francis BRINKLEY a Runing Line to a Gum Tree of Jas THOMAS then a runing Line to apine aCorner Tree o (sic) Robert THOMAS a Runing Line between Jon. ELLIS and Francis BRINKLEY to apine ACorner tree of Jon. ELLIS then aruning Line to apine aCorner tree then aruning Line to a Maple a Corner tree of John ELLIS present James THOMAS and Francis BRINKLEY begining at aHickrey (sic) aCorner tree of Robert NIGHTs (sic) then a Runing Line to Edward HARE Line present William JONES. Begining at a White Oak aCorner Tree of Mary BARNES aruning Line to Edward WARRENs Line present Thomas BARNS beginning at aGum aCorner tree between William GATTLING& Edward HARE aruning Line to a Hickrey a Corner tree of Moses HARE then a runing Line between William GATTLINGs and Moses HARE to aGum a Corner tree Moses ODOMs then aRuning Line

(17) [19] Between William GATTLING and Moses ODOM to aCorner Tree of Moses ODOMs Jur. then a runing Line between Moses ODOM Jur. and William GATTLINGs to aCorner tree aWhite of (sic) Isaac WILLIAMS then a Runing Line between Moses ODAM Junior and Isaac WILLIAMS to the road Present Edward GATLING & William GATLING Junior--beginning at apine aCorner Tree Willis REDDICK then a running line to a Water Oak aCorner tree of William LONG then a running line Between James LONG & Willis REDDICK to the Virginia Line then a running line between Willis REDDICK & Daniel MARCH present William ROGERS & James LONG all these Lines peaseably Processioned

Edward HARE Junior
Joseph SPEIGHT

Aprill 2/d/. Day 1756

In obediance to an order of Vestry we the Subscribers have processioned all the Land Marks we knows of or has been shewed in the District as Laid at (sic) as followeth Between Adam N?ITE and Jacob ODAM in presents Adam NITE And Jacob ODAM and John GREEN & between James EURE and Jacob ODAM in presents James EURE and John GREENBetween Richard PARKER and Mary GREEN in presents John GREEN Senr. and John GREEN Junior Between John SPARKMON and Richard PARKER in presents John SPARKMON and John GREEN and James EURE Between James EURE AndMary GREEN In Presents James EURE and John GREEN and John SPARKMAN in presents John GREEN and James EURE Between James EURE and John SPARKMON in presents John GREEN & James EURE Between Mary GREEN and William SMITH in Presents JohnGREEN and William SMITH Between ElceGREEN and JohnSPARKMON [End of entry. End of page.]

END OF PROCESSION DOCKET

(18) April 5, 1756 Persuant to an Order of the Vestry of St. Pauls Parish we the Subscribers Have processioned all the Land mark (sic) within the Destrict _______ [illegible] Order mentioned as appears by the Li__ [torn] annext Dated April 5/th/. 1756.
William POWELL Richard FELTON
Ent. personed (sic)

(19) [2] Processoned the Line betwean peter pARKER & William tRUEWATHAN both partys Likewise henery mORGAN

Made and Processoned aline for peter pARKER kings Land Joyning henery mORGAN william tRUEWATHAN Present

Porcessoned (sic) the Line betwean the king & william TRUEWATHAN. TRUEWATHAN present Likewise Peter pARKER

Processoned the line between Peter pARKER & Daniel pARKER both parties present Likewise Elijah BENTON

Porcessoned the Line betw__n [torn] Daniel pARKER & The king Daniel pARKER present Likewise William Elijah BENTON

Processoned the Line b_twe_n Eprah__radtus bOYS ___ Richard bAKER both both (sic) pres__t Likewise william TRUEWATHAN

Proc__soned the line betwean John kITTREL & Richard BAKER both parties present Likewise William tRUEW_THAN

Porcessoned ye Line betwean Richard fELTON & Daniel PARKER boht (sic) present Like wise John _INES

Porcessone (sic) the Line betwean Daniel pARKER Richard BAKER both par___s present Likewise william wOTERS

Processon__ ___ [torn] line ______n Richard __KER & peter pARKER both present Like wise ___n? hAINS william wARTERS

Porcessoned the Line betwean Richard BAKER & John hAINS b_th Partys present like wise william wARTERS Daniel pARKER

Porcessoned the Line betwean John kITTREL & John hAINS both partys Present Likewise Richard BAKER and John kITTREL

Porcessoned the Line betwean John hAINS & the king hAINS present Likewise william wORTERS Richard BAKER

(20) Prosistioned (sic) the Line betwen George WILLIAMS and Moses BENTON Present both Parties Present allso Daniel PUGH and John BENTON Son of Moses

Prosistioned the Line betwen Daniel PUGH and George WILLIAMS both Parties Present Likewise Wm. DANIEL John HAMBILTON and John BENTON Jun/r/.

Prosistioned D_n___ PUGH back Line Wm. DANIEL John HAMBITON & George WILLIAMS

Prosistioned the Line Betwen Daniel PUGH and William POWEL Present Bo__ Parties Present Likewise William DANIEL & Henry SMITH

(20) (Cont.) Prosestioned the Line betwen Wm. POWEL & Henry SMITH __th Parties Present Likewise Daniel PUGH Wm. DA?NIEL /&?/ Jonathan BAKER

[Torn]_______ioned the Line __twen Henry SMITH and Daniel PUGH both Parties Present likewise Wm. DANIEL & Jonathan BAKER

Prosestioned the Line betwen Micajah RI?DDICK and Thos. HARRALL both Parties Present Thos. WIGGINS & Richard _ROTHERS and Daniel PUGH

Prosestioned the Line betwen Micajah RIDDICK and Wm. TA?WATHEN Present bo__ _arties Li______ [Torn] D_____ PUGH Thos. WIGGINS and Rich_ BROTHERS

Prosestioned the Line betwen Miajah RIDDICK and Dorathie SMITH Present both Parties Likewise Danl. PUGH Thos. WIGGINS and Richard BROTHERS

Prosestioned the Line betwen Thos HARRAL & Richard FELTON both Parties Present Likewise Wm. DANIEL

(21) [3] Prosestioned the Line betwen William WATERS and Richard BROTHERS both Parties Present Likewise Danl. PUGH and Wm. DANIEL

Prosestioned the Line betwen Richard FELTON & Richard BAKER both Parties Present Likewise Danl. PUGH & John CITTERALL (sic)

Prosestioned the Line betwen John KITTERAL and Richard BAKER both Parties Present likewise Dan/l/. PUGH & Stephen PARKER

Proses___ned the Line betwen John KITTERAL & Wm. WATER both Parties Present Likewise Dan/l/. PUGH and Richard BAKER

Prosestioned the Line betwen Richard BAKER & John KITTERAL both Parties Present Likewise Danl. PUGH [Torn--One full name illegible.] Stephen PARKER

Prosestioned the Line betwen Wm. WATERS and Richard BAKER both Parties /present?/ Likewise Dan_. PUGH & Thos?. BAKER

Prosestioned the Land (sic) betwen Wm. WATERS and Richa_d PARKER both Par___s P___ent Likewise Danl PUGH _____ [Torn.]

Prosestioned the line betwen Richard BAKER and Rich/d/. PARK_R both Parties Present Likewise Dan/l/. PUGH & Thos. WIGGIN_

Prosestioned the Line betwen Epaphaditus BOYCE and R____ BAKER both Parties Present likewise Dan/l/. PUGH & Tos? W__GINS

Prosestioned the line betwen Ric/d/. PARKER & Epaphr?aditus B_YCE both Parties Present Likewise Dan/l/. PUGH & Thos. WIGGINS

Prosestioned the line betwen Daniel PUGH & Epaphraditus both (sic) Pa_ties Present /Likewise/ Richd. BAKER & Thos. WIGGINS

Prosestioned the line betwen Daniel PUGH & Rich/d/. BROTHERS both Parties Present likewise Thos WIGGINS Micajah RIDDICK

Prosestioned the line betwen Daniel PUGH & Elizabeth AL?LEN both Parties Present like-

(21) (Cont.) wise Thos. WIGGINS and Stephen PARKER

Prosestioned the line betwen Daniel PUGH & Wm. WATERS both Parties Present likewise Thos. WIGGINS & Andrew MATTHEWS

(22) Pros__tioned the line betwen Daniel PUGH and Thos. WIGGENS both Parties Present likewise Wm. WATERS & Andrew MATTHEWS

Prosestioned the line betwen Daniel PUGH and Wm. HUGHES Daniel PUGH Present Wm. HUGHS Refusing or Negleting (sic) Present Moses BENTON George WILLIAMS & Jessee WIL____S

Prosesoned (sic) the line btwen John bENTON & Moses PARKER John bENTON present

Processioned the Line btwean (sic) John bENTON _ Calleb POLSON present James PARKER Elijah BENTON

Processored the Line betwea?n the king & James PARKER present Elijah bENTON Calleb pOLSON

Percessored the Line btwean John WILLIAMSON & James PARKER both present Elijah BENTON Calleb pOLSON

Porcessored the Line /betwen?/ the King & John wILLAMSON John? wILLIAMSON present James PARKER present

Porcessoned the line betw___ James PARKER & Elijah bENTON both partys present

Procesoned the Line /betwean/ Dorthy SMITH & William TRUEWATHAN both present Like wise amos SMITH

Processoned the Line betwean Dorithy SMITH & __m?uel POWELL both present Likewise peter pARKER

Processoned the Line Dorthy SMITH & henery mOR_AN both part__s present Like wise peter pARKER

Processoned the Line betwean henery mORGAN & ______ POWELL both partys present Likewise peter pARKER

Prossoned (sic) the Line betwean Lemuell POWELL william TREUEWATHAN both present Like wise peter pARKER

Processoned a line for William TRUEWATHAN present Peter PARKER henery mORGAN

(23) Porcessoned the line betwean Ephroditus bOYS & William wATERS present both parties likewise Daniel PARKER John hAINS

Porcessoned the line betwean John kITTREL & william hUGGS (sic) John kITTREL present william hUGGS neglecting or Refusing present George kITTREL Jesse wILLIAMS

Porssoned the tine betwean John kITTREL Jane wILLIAMS both parties present Likewise George kITTREL

Processoned the line betwean willium hUGGS & Jan/e/ WILLIAMS Both parties present

(23) (Cont.) Porcessoned the line Betwean william hUGGS & mary vANN Both present

porcessoned the Lines /of/ William hUGHS all but one marked after they ware for warn by John kITTREL

porcessoned the Lines John VANNN him present

Porcessoned a__ ___ [Blot] all the Lines mary vANN She poressted (sic)

Porcessoned the Line betwean mary SOWARD & George wILLIAMS both present Likewise Joseph fIGG

Porcessoned the line betwean george wILLIAMS & the king George wILLIAMS present Likewise Joseph fIGG

Porcessoned the line betwean mary SOWARD & the king George wILLIAMS presemt

Porcessoned the Line betwann (sic) mary SOWARD & Laranc (sic) BAKER both present Like wise ~~william~~ George wILLIAMS

Porcessoned the Line Larance bAKER & and (sic) the king Larance BARKER (sic) present Likewise William DANIEL

Porcessoned the Line of John LUIS (sic) Edward vANN present

Processioned the Line Between Abraham LACITOR & my Lord present ===== /the/ parties & John BRINKLEY & Elijah BENTON

Processioned the Line Between Elijah BENTON & Abraham LACITOR present Both parties, Elijah BIRD & John WEBB Likewise

Processioned the Line Between Elijah BENTON & Lemuel POWEL present Elijah BENTON

(24) In abeadence (sic) to athorety we have Processioned all ___ _ands that Was Laid out and Apinted for us to Do--

Feb ___ 17__ Edward WARREN his Land Dun Demsey RUCKES his La__ Dun present Edward VANN and Joseph WAREN Edward VANN his Land Dun Jeames BRADEY Land Dun present Jacob RUCKS Edward VANN & Jeames BRADEY

_eb/r/ 9/th/.. _756 _____ RUCKS his Land dun prsent Demsey RUCKS & Jacob RUCKS Jeams BRADY & Jacob ODOM

Febr 10/th/. 1756 Jeams ELLIS Seaner his land dun Jeams ELLIS Juner his Land dun Jeames BAKER his Land Dun Samuel BAKER his Land Dun present Jeames ELLIS Jeams BAKER Richard BAKER John ODOM

Feb/r/. ye 10/th/. 1756 Wm. GONES his Land Dun John ODOM his Land Dun Jeathro HARREL his Land Dun present John ODOM and Wm. GONES Roberd KNIGHT Jeames ELLIS Jethro HARREL

feb/r/. 11/th/: John pARKE/R/ his Land Dun John PARKER his Other Land Dun present John pARKER John ODOM Jeames ELLIS

febuary (sic) ye. 14/th/ 1756 Roberd ROGERS his Land Dun Henery GOODMONS his Land Dun Joel== GOODMON his Land Dun Jeams BRADY his Land Dun Edward WARREN his Land Dun

(24) (Cont.) Isaac pIPKEN his Land Dun Wm. GOODMON present Henery GOODMON Roberd ROGERS Joel GOODMON Edward WARREN Isaac pIPKEN Wm. GOOD MON (sic)

[Note: Portions of the edges and center of this sheet are missing.] febuary 14/th/. 1756 Wm. SMITH h__ ____ _un frances BRI_____ _is Land dun present fran___ BRINKLEY Roberd J___S Wm. SMI__ _____ TOMIS (sic) W______ ______ Roba?rd KN____s ___ Land dun Jeames ELLIS ____ his Land dun present Rober_ __IGHT Wm.. fELTEN Jeams ELLIS

feb 25? ==Thomas LANGSTONs Land un (sic) frances LANGSTONs Land dun present Roberd KNIGHT Wm. fELTEN Thomas LANGSTON

febr. 27/th/. 1756 John ODOM his __nd dun present Edward WARREN

febr 27/th/. 1756 Edward HARE h__ Land dun John LEWIS his Land dun Joseph BRADE_ his Land dun John DUKINS his Land Dun Elizebath hART LOCK hur Land dun present Edward hARE John LEWIS Joseph BRADY John DUCKINS Elezebath hART ___K

febuary 28/th/. 1756 Roberd ROGERS his Land dun Stephen ROGERS his Land dun Thomas LANG_____ his Land dun present Rober_ ___ERS Stephen ROGERS Thoma_ ___GSTON

Feb/r/ 28/th/. 1756 John PARKER h__ ___d dun Wm. UMFLEET ___ _and dun present John _____ER Wm. UMFLEET Thom? _____

feb/r/. 28/th/ 1756 Thomas hARRE_Es his Land dun Jeames BRADYs &? Wm? GOODMANs Lands Dun Elexander CARTE_ ___ Land dun present Stephen ROGERS Elexander CARTER

March the 2/d/. 1756 John ODOM his Land Dun Thomas HARRELEs his Land dun Ephrititus GONES his Land dun Je/a/thro HARRELL his Land dun Jeames ELLIS his Land dun John ODOMs Swamp Dun present Ephrititus GONES Jethro HAR____ John ODOM Jacob ODOM Joseph TOM?___

March 11/th/.. 1756 Willis REDDICK his Land Dun Stephen SHEPARD Two Tracks Dun Jacob ODOM his Land dun Edward VANN (or VAUN) his Land Dun present Willis REDDICK Stephen SHEPARD Joseph NOFLEETT (sic) Daniel LAS?_____

March 16/th/: 1756 Roberd TOMIS his Land Dun Jeames TOMIS his Land Dun frances BRINKLEY Land Dun Present Roberd TOMIS & Jeanes TOMIS & frances BRINKLEY

[No date.] Thomas PILAND his Land dun Edward PILAND his Land Dun Joseph NOFLEET present Thomas PILAND Edward PILAND Jeames PILA__ Joseph NOFLEET

March 26/th/.. 1746 Gorge (sic) VANN his Land dun Jacob ====VANN his Land Du_ present Gorge VAN Jacob ROGE__ Jacob VANN Elezebath VANN

March ye 29th: 1746 Henery BACKER (sic) his Land Dun a__ his Mill Joynding (sic) to NOFLET present Joseph NOFLEET Henery BAKER Jeames Bray BAKER

(25) ____e?___ ____: 1756 Edward HARE Juner his Land Dun Philip PIPKINS his Land Dun Moses ODOM Land Dun present Edward HARE Isaac pIPKIN Moses ODOM

[No date.] Moses HARE his Land dun Isaac WILLIAMES his Land Dun present Moses hARE Isaac WILLIAMS

febuary 25/th/ 1756 Edward HARE his Land Dun Edward HARE his Land Dun (sic) Isaac WILLIAMS his Land dun present Edward HARE Isaac WILLIAMS Stueard (sic) PIPKIN his Land

(25) (Cont.) dun Stephen SHEPARD his Land dun Roberd pARKER his land dun present Stuard pIPKIN ~~Stuard~~ Stephen SHEPARD and Roberd PARKER

_arch __/th/. _756 Edward hAREs his other land dun Jeames CONNER his Land dun present Edward hARE Jeanes CONER

____h ___ _____56 Jacob ODOM his Land dun Joseph KNOWFLEET his land dun Jeames EUREE his land dun present Joseph kNOWFLEET Thomas LANGSTONEs Thoms PILAND his land dun Wm. fRIER his land dun

___ch _6/th/ _756 Roberd KNIGHT & Wm. =GONES There Land Dun present Gorge vAN Jacob ODOM Roberd KNIGHT John PORTER his land d__

A Cording to the Order of Veastery (sic) We have processioned all ye Land That is within ____ Bou___ P_os_ioned by us Jacob ODOM
Jeames BRADEY
Ent.

(26) January the 10th. 1756
Processioned Parsuant to order, by Abner EASON & Guy HILL Lines Between Thomas WALTON and Nathinel (sic) SPIVEY
Between Nathinel SPIVEY and Jacob SPIVEY
Between Jacob SPIVEY and Aron HILL Junr..
Between Jacob SPIVEY and Aron HILL Senr.
Between Timothy WALTON and Aron HILL Senr.
Between Micaiath (sic) BLANCHARD and Aron HILL Snr.
Between Aron HILL Snr. and Aron HILL Junr.
Between Jacob SPIVEY and Epharim BLANCHARD
Between Epharim BLANCHARD and Beniamin BLANCHARD
Between Micaiath BLANCHARD and Beniamin BLANCHARD
Between Amous BLANCHARD and Aron BLANCHARD
Between James GRIFFIN and Joseph GRIFFIN
Between James GRIFFIN and Abraham HILL
Between James GRIFFIN and Guy HILL
Between Guy HILL and Jonas SPIVEY
Between Jonas SPIVEY and James GRIFFIN
Between Jonas SPIVEY and Joal SPIVEY
Between Joal SPIVEY and Moses ROUNTREE
Between Joal SPIVEY and Abraham HILL
Between Joal SPIVEY and Edward BEREYMAN
Between George EASON and Beniamin BEREYMAN
Between Samuel STALLINGS and James SCOT
Between George EASON and James SCOT
Between James SCOT and Beniamin BEREYMAN
Between George EASON and Beniamin BEREYMAN
Between George EASON and Abner EASON
Between Abner EASON and Edward BEREYMAN
Between Abner EASON and Guy HILL
Between Guy HILL and Abraham HILL
Between Abraham HILL and Edward BEREYMAN
Between Guy HILL and Moses ROUNTREE
Between John EVENS and Joseph GRIFFIN
Between Joseph GRIFFIN and William WALTON
Between William WALTON and Edward TROTMON
Between Edward TROTMAN and Moses ROUNTREE

(27) Between Jacob DOCTON and Moses PEARCE
Between Luke SUMNER and Joal HUNTOR
Between Elisha HUNTOR and William HUNTOR
Between Elisha HUNTOR and Samuel GREEN
Between Samuel GREEN and William EASON
Between William EASON and Joseph HURDLEE
Between Joseph HURDLEE and Jacob DOCTON
Between Isaac SPEIGHT and George EASON Senr.

Persuant to anOrder of Vestry Dated the 15/th/ of October 1755 We the Subscribers have processioned all the Lands within the Destrict mentioned in the Said Order as by aboveList Dated the 6th of April 1756 pr Abner EASON
Guy HILL
Ent/d/. Ent/d/.

(28) North Carolina Chowan Count (sic) April ye 5th 1756
Persuant to an order of Vestry ~~held~~ past== the 25th of October 1755. Wee the subscribers being appounted processioners to procession a Canton laid out for them by the s/d/. Vestry beginning att BENNETs Creek Bridg (sic) so along BENNETs Creek Road to Cathries (sic) Creek Bridg so down the s/d/. Creek to the River thence up the River to BENNETs Creek thence up the s/d/ Creek to the afors/d/. Bridg. and accordingly we met & qualified and then processioned all the Lands within the s/d/. Canton only Mr James WILSON & Mr Henry HILL Refused to procession with Jesse HUNTOR. and Edward pEYLAND refuses to procession with James WILSON Benjaman BLANSHARD
Jesse HUNTOR

(29) January the 29/th/. 1756 Prosesioned (sic) for William GOODMAN begining at a pine a fore & aft tree In A Runing (sic) Line to a pine a Corner tree between Wm GOODMAN & Wm. LANG a Runing Line to a pine a Corner tree a Runing Line to a gum a Corner tree a Runing Line to a pine a Corne (sic) tree of James LANG present Robert ROGERS & John WEE?B A runing Line betwen Wm. GOODMAN and Robert ROGERS to a pine a Corner Tree of Wm. GOODMAN a runing Line to the road present Isaac pIPKIN & Robert ROGERS prosesioned for Isaac PIPKIN a runing Lin (sic) to the Run of the bever dam to a pin a Corner tree of Isaac PIPKINs A runing Line betwene Wm. GOODMAN & Isaac PIPKIN to the Road Present Wm. GATTLING Ju/r/. & Jo/n/. WEBB begining at the Senter Three pines /of Thos. bARNS a Runing Line to the Sente (sic) of three pines of John WINBOURNs Line a Runing Line to a Red Oak a Corne tree of Frances BRINKLEY Line to a White Oak a Corner Tree of John ODOM Line a Runing Line to a pine a Corne Tree of John ODOMs Present John SKINER & Jacob ODOM a runing Line from A red Oak to a Pine a Corner tree of Thomas BARNSes a runing Line Betwene Jo/n/. ODOM & Thos. BARNES to the Senter of three Trees Present Jo/n/. SKINER & Jacob ODOM begining at a White Oak a Corner Tree of Ja/s/. THOMAS a runing Line to a White oak a Corner Tree then a Runing line to a White Oak a Corner tree of John SKINE_ then a Runing Line to a branch Present Ja/s/. ODOM Jo/n/. ODOM & Wm. FELTON Ju/n/. begining at a Water Oak a Corne tree of Frances BRINKLEY a runing Line to a gum a Corner tree of Ja/s/. THOMA_ then a Runing Line to a pine a Corner Tree o (sic) Robert THOMAS A Runing Line betwene Jo/n/. ELLIS & Frances BRINKLEY to a pine

(30) A Corner tree of Jo/n/: ELLES then a Runing Line to a pine a Corne tree then a runing Line to a Maple a Corne tree of John ELLIS preesent James THOMAS & Frances BRINKLEY begining at a Hickrey a Corner Tree of Robert NIGHT's (sic) then a runing Line to Edward HARE Line present Wm JONES? begining at a Whit (sic) Oak a Corner Tree of mary BARNES a Runing Lin to Edward WARRENs Line present Thomas BARNES begining at a gum a Corner tree betwen Wm. GATTLING & Edward HARE a runing Line to a hickrey a Corner tree of Moses hARE then a runing Line betwene Wm. GATLING & Moses HARE to a Gum a

(30) (Cont.) Corne tree Moses ODOMs then a runin (sic) Line Betwen Wm. GATTLING & moses ODOM to a Corne tree of Moses ODOMs Ju/r/ then a runing Line betwen Moses ODOM Jur. and Wm. GATTLING to a Corner tree a White of (sic) Isaac WILLIAMS then a runing Line betwen Moses ODOM Ju/r/. & Isaac WILLIAM (sic) to the Road present Edward GATTLING & Wm. GATLING Juner begining at at (sic) a pine a Corner tree Willes RIDDICK then a runing Line to a Water Oak & a Co/rner/ tree of Wm. LANG then a runing Line betwen James LANG & Willes RIDDICK to the Virgina (sic) Line then a runing Line betwen Willis RIDDICK & Dainel (sic) MARCH present Wm. ROGERS & James LANG all these Lines Peasabely (sic) Prosesioned

Edward HARE Ju/r/.
Joseph SPEIGHT

(31) April /th/. 2. Day 1756
In Obdance (sic) to an order of Vestry we the Subscriders have ~~por~~/r/cessined (sic) all the Lands marks we knows of or has bin show/e/ed in the Destrict us Laid == att (sic) as folleweth Betwene Adam NITE and Jacob ODOM ~~and~~ in presants Adam NITE and Jacob ODOM and John gREEN & Betwene James EURE and Jacob ODOM in presants Janes EURE and Jacob ODOM & William UMFLET Betwene Mary gREEN and Jacob ODOM in presonts James EURE and Joseph gREN (sic) Betwene Richard pARKER and Mary gREEN in presents John gREEN Snr. and Joh_ gREEN Jun/r/: Betwene John SPARKMON and richard pARKOR in presonts John SP__KMON and and (sic) John gREEN and James EURE: Betwene Janes EURE and Mary gR___ In presonts James EURE and John gREEN and John SPARKMON Betwene John gREEN and John SPARKMON in presonts John gREEN and James EURE Betwene James EURE and John SPARKMON in presonts John gREEN and James EURE Betwene == Mary gREEN and William SMITH in presonts ~~Jeth~~ ? John gRE/E/N and william SMITH Betwene Else GREEN and Thomas SPARKMON in presonts Thomas pARKMO/N/ (sic) & John gREN and William SMITH Betwene Else gREEN and William fELTON in presonts John gREEN and Thomas SPARKMON & William SMITH Betwene William fELTON and Thomas SPARKMON in presonts william fELTON and Thomas SPAR/KMO/_ and William SMITH Betwene Thomas HARRELL and Thomas SPARKMON in presonts Thomas SPARKMON and Thomas HARRELL and William fELTON Betwene Thomas HARRELL and william fILTON In presonts Thomas HARRELL and William fILTON and Wiliam SMITH Betwene William SMITH and Soloman gREEN in presonts Soloman gREEN and William SMITH and Jonathan SM/A/L? Betwene Soloman gREEN and Thomas NORIS (sic) in presonts Soloman gREEN and Thomas NORIS and William SMITH Betwene James EURE /Jur/ and Thomas NORIS in presonts Thomas NORIS and James EURE Betwene Thomas NORIS and Sam==muell (sic) EURE in presonts Sammuell EURE and Thomas NORIS and James EURE Betwene Samuell EURE and Andrew HAMBLONTON (sic) presonts Samuell EURE and Andrew HAMBLETON and Thomas NORIS Betwene James EURE and Andrew HAMBLETON in prsonts James EURE and Andrew hAMBLETON & Thomas NORIS Betwene Andrew hAMBLETON and Williuam UMFLET in presonts William UMFET and Andrew hAMBLETON and Thomas HARELL Betwene James EURE and William UMFLET part le don (sic) in presonts James EURE and William UMFLET and Thomas HARRELL Betwene Thomas HARRELL ___ Epaproditus JONS (sic) part don in presonts Thomas HARRELL and Epaproditus JONS and John ODOM Betwen Epaproditus JONES and John ODOM in presonts John ODOM and Epaproditus JONES and Jacob ODOM Betwne Jethro HARRELL and Epaproditus JONES /part don/ in presonts Jethro HARRELL and Epaproditus /JONS/ and John ODOM and Jacob ODOM and ~~Fosph~~ Joseph TOMAS (sic)

(32) Betwene Thomas HARRELL and John gREEN in presonts Thomas HARRELL and John gREEN and Thomas SPARKMON Betwene Thomas HARRELL and Mary gREEN in presonts Thomas HARRELL and John gREEN and Thomas SPARKMON Betwene mary gREEN and Soloman gREEN in presonts Solomon gREEN & James EURE Betwene Solomon ~~and~~ gREEN and Jonas TALER in presents Soloman gREEN and Jonas TALER and Willam TOMAS Betwene John gREEN and Jonas TALER in presonts Jonas TALER and Solomon gREEN Betwene William LANCTON and Jonas TALER ~~and Soloman~~ /in/ ~~gREEN~~ presonts William LANCTON and Jonas TALER and Soloman gREEN Betwene William TOMAS and Jonas TALER in presonts Jonas TALER and William TOMAS and Soloman gREEN Betwene William LANCTON and Mary gREEN in presonts William LANCTON and Jonas

(31) (Cont.) and Jonas TALER and William LANCTON Betwene John BUTLER and Lunard LANCTON in presonts William LANCTON and Lunard LANCTON and Jonas TALER Betwene John dENVA (sic) in presonts Lonard LANCTON and Jonas TALER Betwene John DENVE and Thomas LANCTON in presonts Jonas TALER Betwene Tomas LANCTON and Epaproditus JONS in presents Eparaditus (sic) JONS and Larnnel? LANCTON and Lunard LANCTON Betwene James ELLIS and ~~Eprod~~? Epaproditus JONS in presonts James ELLIS and Epaproditus JONS Betwene Edard SKETER and Larance LANSTON in presonts Larance LANSTON and Lunard LANSTON and James EURE ~~Joseph NORFLET~~ Betwene Jose/p/h NORFLET and Edard SKETER in pres/o/___ Jacob ODOM and Joseph NORFLET and James fRIER Betwene Joseph NORFLET and John ODOM in presonts Joseph NORFLET and Jacob ODOM and James fRIER Betwene John ODOM and Jacob ODOM in presonts Jacob ODOM and Joseph NORFLET and James fRIER, Betwene ____ [Torn] Edard ARNAL and Jacob ODOM in presonts Jacob ODOM and James fRIER and Joseph NORFLET Betwene Jacob ODOM and John SIMON in presonts Jacob ODOM and Joseph NORFLET and James fRIER Betwene John fOLK and Charls RUSIL in presonts James EURE and Lunard LANSTON Betwene Charls RUSIL and John WORIL in presonts James EURE and Lunard LANSTON Betwene John WORIL and John CLITTLIN in presonts John CITLON (sic) and John WORIL and John CARTER and Tomas SPARKMON betwene John CITLON and James BRADY in presonts Jacob ODOM and Tomas SPARKMON and John CITLON Betwene John KITTERLON and John CARTER in presonts John KITTERLON & and (sic) John CARTER and Jacob ODOM and Stephen EURE Betwene Stphen EURE and John KITTERLON in presonts Stphen EURE and John KITTERLON and Joseph NORFLET and John CARTER Betweene Stphen EURE and Henry SKINER in presonts Stphen EURE and Thomas LANCTON and John CARTER and Thomas SPARKMON Betwene John CARTER and ~~John~~ Henry SKINER in presonts John CARTER and Thomas SPARKMON and Tomas LANSTON Betwene James EURE and Tomas LANSTON in presonts Lunard LANSTON and James EURE all Concluded Within my Bounds Excepting Two or Thre (sic) Tracks in ye Precoson be Longing to Sum Persons I kow (sic) not all above Duley and Peasibley Dun With Consent in the Presence of Us

Jeathro HARRELL
Janes ~~EVANS~~? EURE

(32) At a Vestry Held for St: Pauls Parish at CONSTANTs Chappel on Satterd. the 25.the (sic) Day of October 1755. It was Then and There Pursuant to the Law for Settleing The Title and Bounds of Peoples Lands Ordered That Mr: Robert RODGERS and Mr John ARLINE be and they are hereby Appointed Processioners and that They do Procession all The Lands Included begining near Moses PARKERs on The New Road so along The Said Road to The Road at Sarum Chappel so along Sarum Road to The Cuntry Line & along ye Line to The NewRoad (sic), And That They make Return Thereof To the County Court in April next According to Law. Which they are not to Omit under The Penalty of Five Pounds Each, &c- Luke SUMNER. Clk Vty:

Copy.

(33) Jemewary (sic) the 26 Sessoned (sic) for Peter PARKER Willm DOUTE Moses BOIS Preasent John MORE Peter PARKER Grigory GHOUGH

February the 4 day Sessoned for John BATHA Demce ODAHAMS and tha (sic) John CONOR? lines on Preasen/t/ William HUGHS John BATHA Jhn CONER

Janewary the 14 day [End of entry.]

Begun ienew (sic) on the 24 to Procession went not Lines John BATHA Samuel === WALIS? Lemel ODAHAM BATHA and ODAHAM Not a Greed (sic)

Sessioned the 27? For John WATER for Nickolas KIN/G/ par_tal? Sesson ther (sic) lines John KITTERAL Nickola?s KING Samuel wILLIAM/S/ preasent
Order of Vestry Robert RODGERS & John ARLINE Processioners &c

[No date]

(34) (Cont.) lines John KITTEREL Nickoli?s KING Samuel wILLIAM/S/ preasent Order of Vestry.Robert RODGERS.& John ARLINE Processioners &c

(35) There present Moses hARE and Aaron ODAM processiond the Line between them Begining at a pine there Corner tree then a Long the Line of marked trees to moses hARE/s/ tother (sic) Corner pine there present John DRURY and Aaron /oDAM/ And Abraham oDAM processiond the Line Between John DRURY and Aaron oDAM to the Center of three oaks-- Then processiond the Line between John DRURY and Abraham oDAM to a Corner white oak near the Road.-- Then present Daniel mARCH and Abraham oDAM procesiond the Line between them from a Red oak there Line tree along the Line to a Corner pine Aarons ODAMs Corner pine & then a Long the Line between Aaron ODAM and abraham ODAM to the Center of three oaks-- Then present Daniel mARCH and Aaron oDAM processiond the Line from Aaron ODAMs Corner pine along the Line between them two to a Corner pine John wEEBs (sic) Corner processiond to the Short beaver Dam then up the beaverdam to a Line of marked trees to Fru/r/ (sic) MORIESs Corner then a Line of marked trees to the Grate beaver dam present Aaron ODAM then present moses HARE and Edward HARE processiond the Line between them two from a Corner hickry a Long the Line to a Corner pine-present Edward hARE and John LEWIS processiond the Line between them two from a Corner Gum to a Gum a Corner tree on mILSes Swamp-present Thomas BARNS and Francis SANDERS processiond the Line for Thomas BARNS from a Gum his Corner tree then a Long his Line to the Center of three pines then a Long his Line to a white oak his Corner tree-- Present Henry KING processiond the Line Between he & Thomas BARNS Begining at a pine KINGs Corner tree then a Long the Line to a Gum &? KINGs Corner tree-present Henry KING processiond his Line begining at A Small dead Gum his Corner tree then along his Line to a pine moses hAREs Corner tree then a Long KINGs Line to his one Corner tree A white Oak-present moses hARE and francis SANDERS processiond the Line Between Joseph SPEIGHT and henry KING begining at a Red oak a Corner tree then a Long the Line to the head Line then along that to the Long Branch-

(36) then present moses hARE and francis SANDERS processiond the Line for moses hARE Begining at a pine on the Side of the flat Cyprus So Down the Sand Banks along a Line of marked trees to the Road-present moses hARE & william SPEIGHT processiond begining at a white Oak A Corner tree betwen them two then along the Line to a Corner pine then along the Line to HAREs Corner tree present william SPEIGHT and Francis SANDERS processi/ond/ the Line for farncis (sic) SANDERS begining at a Red oak his Corner then along his Line to a white oak his Corner then a Long his Line to a white oak his Corner tree-present John wOLLICE (sic) and Charles KING processiond for John wOLLICE begini/n/g att his Corner Gum then a long his Line to his Corner white oak then along his Line to bOIYCEs line then a Long there Line to Charles KINGs Corner-then present Charles KING and Christopher bOIYCE processiond the Line between them two from KING Corner along the Line to EVERITs Corner pine then along KINGs Line of marked trees to his one Corne/r/ then present Charles KING and francis SANDERS & Christophe bOIYCES processiond bOIYCEs Line from EVERITs Corner pine along his Line to his one Corner pine then a Long his Line to hINTERs Corner then a Long the Line of marked trees to WOLICEs Line then present John wOLICE processiond the Line for him from a white oak his Corner a long his Line of marked trees to a Swamp Caled the Gum Swa__ [Torn] then present william LANG and John wEEB James LANG processiond the Line btween william LANG and James LANG from a Corner pine along the Line of marked trees to the Corner a pine between James LANG and william GOODMAN to a Corner Red oak Robert ROGERSes Corner present James LANG and John BETHEY processiond the Line between them two to a pine on Sarum Road then along the Line betwee (sic) Trustum bETHEY and James LANG to a hickry there Corner and then a Long the Line between them two to a pine one (sic) the Beatch Swamp there Corner tree

(37) present William SPEIGHT processiond for Joseph SPEIGHT his Line from a pine

[No date]

(37) (Cont.) ~~James WIGINGs~~ /willm hARRISONs/ Corner along the Line to the miry Branch to a pine-present ~~Edwaren~~ Edward wAREN and John LEWES processiond the Line between Joseph SPEIGHT and John LEWIS from A white oak and Gum to the Center of thre pines-then present Thomas BARNS and Edward wARREN processiond the Line Betwee (sic) Joseph SPEIGHT and Edward wARREN from the Center of three pines to a Corner pine SPEIGHTs Corner-then present Thomas BARNS Processiond the Line between Joseph SPEIGHT & Thomas BARNS from SPEIGHTs Corner a Long the Line to BARNSes Corne oak then a Long the Line to BARNES Corner a pine in KINGs Line-then present Edward hARE & John LEWIS processiond the Line Between John LEWIS and Edward WARREN from the Center of three pines along the line to wARRENs Corner pine-Then present Ed hARE and Ed wARREN & Thomas BARNS processiond for Ed HARE and Ed wARREN from a Corner pine a Long the Line of marked trees to an oak-Then present Charles KING and henry KING processiond the Line Between Joseph SPEIGHT & Charles KING begining at a pine a Corner of KINGs then aLong the Line of marked trees to a white oak SPEIGHT Corner then a Long the Line to a white oak SPEIGHT outher Corner-then present Francis SANDERS & Henry KING and Ed HARE processiond the Line between Joseph SPEIGHT & Francis SANDERS begining at a Gum SPEIGHTs Corner tree then aLong the Line of marked trees to the Road-present ~~Jas~~ William VAUGHN processiond for him Begining at a maple his Corner then a Long his Line to his outher Corner pine then aLong his Line to a popler his Corner then a Long his Line ~~to a~~ the Gum Swamp-

(38) All these Lines Peasably Prosesioned

Edward HARE Jur:
Joseph SPEIGHT

1764/1765

(39) In Obedience to an Order of Vestry Dated October the 23/rd/. 1764 We the Posessioners have Processioned all the Land between the flat Branch and the Contrey (sic) line, and along BENNETs Creek to the main Road

Lines Between whom,	Who Present
Luke SUMNER & Sam/el/: SUMNER	the parties present
Sam/el/ SUMNER & Elisha SUMNER under Age	one party & Luke SUMNER
Jacob SUMNER & Willis WIGGINS	one party & Moses HARREL
Edward ARNELL & Eliz/th/. KNIGHT	both Parties
Eliz/th/: KNIGHT & Willis WIGGINS	one Party & Edward ARNELL
Edward ARNELL & Joseph JONES	one Party & Tho/s/: PARKER
Tho/s/: PARKER & Edward ARNELL	one Party & Joseph JONES
Edward ARNELL & Willis WIGGINS	the Parties
Edward ARNELL & James PARKER	one Party & John DARDEN
John DARDEN & Willis WIGGINS	one Party & Edward ARNELL
John DARDEN & James PARKER	one Party & Edward ARNELL

Lines	Who Present
James JONES (sic) & John GORDON	the parties
David JONES & Peter BRINKLEY	the Parties
David JONES & Eliz/th/. NORFLEET	the Parties
Tho/s/: PARKER & Moses HARE	the Parties
Tho/s/: PARKER & William PARKER	one Party and Moses HARE
Epa/ts/: BENTON & James PARKER	the Parties
Epa/ts/: BENTON & Tho/s/: PARKER	one Party & Moses BENTON
Epa/ts/: BENTON & Jethro BENTON	the Parties
Jethro BENTON & Isaac BENTON	one Party & Moses BENTON
Isaac BENTON & John REED	one Party & Rob/t/: PEALE
Joseph BRINKLEY & Kader BALLARD under Age Joseph BRINKLEY	one Party & Elisha NORFLEET

(39) (Cont.)

Edward ARNELL & Joseph JONES	one Party & Tho/s/: PARKER
Joseph JONES & William PARKER	the Parties
Willis WIGGINS & Tho/s/ FRAZIER	the Parties
Demsey SUMNER & John DARDEN	the Parties
Demsey SUMNER & James PARKER	the Parties
Jethro BENTON & Epaphroditus BENTON	the Parties
Isaac BENTON & Robert PEALE	the Parties
Robert PEALE & John REED	one Party & Isaac BENTON
Francis POWELL & James JONES	one Party
& Marmaduke NORFLEET	one Party & Elisha NORFLEET
Joseph BRINKLEY & David JONES	the Parties
Joseph BRINKLEY & Eliz/th/: NORFLEET	the Parties
David JONES & Marmaduke NORFLEET	one Party & Peter BRINKLEY
Marmaduke NORFLEET & John GORDON	the Parties
John GORDON & William POWELL	the Parties
Francis POWELL & Peter BRINKLEY	John GORDON & Demsey JONES
Francis POWELL & William POWELL	John SLAVING? Demsey JONES
Mark:/e?/ NORFLEET & Jethro BALLARD under Age	one Party
David JONES & Moses hARE	the Parties

Carried over

(40) Lines Between whom Who Present

Lines Between whom	Who Present
David JONES & Eliz/th/: NORFLEET	the Parties
Moses HARE & Eliz/th/: NORFLEET	the Parties
Bidgit WIGGENS & James JONES	the Parties
Bridget WIGGENS & Rob/t/: PEALE	the Parties

Jacob NORFLEET
his
David ?? JONES Processioners
mark

(41) Oct/r/. 23/d/. 1764 ordered that Isaac HARREL and Davi_ RICE Do procession all the Lands from the Loosing Swamp Down Perquimons Road /to/ SPEIGHTs Plantation thence by the Cart Road that Leads to Elisha HUNTERs Then Down /by/ Meherin Swamp to BENNETs Creek and up the Creek to the Flat Branch then by the Loosing Swamp ~~to the flat Branch~~ perquimons Road and make Return thereof to April Court Next According to Law Abraham NORFLEET Clk vestry

(42) [On back] For Mr. David RICE or Mr Isaac HARREL

(43) North Carolinar Chowan County April ye 6/th/ 1765
Possesioned (sic) Lines Between Elisha HUNTER and John GORDEN Between Jacob HUNTER and John GORDEN Betwee_ Jacob HUNTER and James JONES Between Jacob HUNTER and Elizabeth HARRILL Between James JONES and Moses MEAZELS Between James JONES and Elizabeth RICE Between James JONES and Isaac SPIGHT Between Abraham HARRILL and Isaac SPIGHT Between John GORDEN and Thomas FULENTON Between John GORDEN and George EASON Between Isaac

(43) (Cont.) SPIGHT and Aaron LACITER Between David RICE and Samuel HARRILL Between Isaac HARRILL and Samuell HARRILL Between Aaron LACITER and Samuell HARRILL Between David RICE and Elizabeth HARRILL Between David RICE and Aaron LACITER Between Aaron LACITER and Elizabeth RICE Between James JONES and Elizabeth RICE Between James JONES and Abrm.. HARRILL Between Aaron LACITER and Abraham HARRILL Between William HINTON and Abram.. HARRILL Between Aaron LACITER and William HINTON Between Aaron LACITER and Thos FULENTON Between William HINTON and Thomas FULENTON Between John BRIGGS and Thomas FULENTON Between William HINTON and John BRIGGS Between Aaron LACITER and Elizabeth RICE Between Isaac HARRILL and Aaron LACITER Between Isaac HARRILL and David RICE Between James JONES and John JONES Between Josiah GRANBERY and John JONES Between Josiah GRANBERY and James JONES Between James JONES and Elizabeth RICE Between Josiah GRANBERY and Elizabeth RICE Between Samuell HARRILL and Elizabeth RICE Between Josiah GRANBERY and Samuell HARRILL

Carried over

(44) Between Josiah GRANBERY and William HINTON Between Josiah GRANBERY and John DAVIS Between Josiah GRANBERY and Hugh HILL Between Josiah GRANBERY and Robert POWELL Between Moses SPIGHT and William HINTON Between William HINTON and James FELPS Between Moses SPIGHT and William SPIGHT Between the Land Formerly belonging to Daniel PUGH and William WALTON and Robert LACITER and William BOND and William SPIGHT Between John DAVIS and Hugh HILL Between John DAVIS and John BRIGGS Between Thomas SMALL and John BRIGGS Between Thomas SMALL and Jesse EASON Between John BRIGGS and James JONES Tayler Between Luke SUMNER and James JONES ta (sic) Between Jesse EASON and Thomas FULENTON Between John bRIGS and Luke SUMNER Between Robert POWELL and Frances POWEL Between Robert POWELL and Moses SPIGHT Between Robert POWELL and Hugh HILL Between Robert POWELL and Luke SUMNER: Between the Land Formerly belonging to Daniel PUGH and Robert POWELL and Moses SPIGHT and Willis JONES and James FELPS Between Willis JONES and James FELPS Between William SPIGHT and James FELPS

Agreable to an order of Vestry Hereunto Enexd (sic) we the Subscribers have processioned all the Lines in our District From the Loosing Swamp Down Pequimons Road to SPIEKSes (sic) Plantation thence by the Cart Road that Leads to Mr. HUNTORs Down Meherin Swamp to bENETs Creek up the Creek to the flat Branch then by the Losing Swamp to pequimons Road

David RICE
Isaac HARRILL

(45) octr. 23/d/: 1764 Ordered that William BOND and Palatiah WALTON Do procession all the Lands that are included From Meherin Swamp Begining at Jacob HUNTERs mill up the Said Swamp to the Piping Branch So along the Said Branch to the main road And __wn the said road to Aaron BLANSH_RDs old Road and alo__ the Said old Road to BENNETs Creek road up the Said Road to BENNETs Creek Bridge and thence up BENNETs Creek to the Mill on Meherin Swamp and make Return thereof to April Court Next according to Law

Abraham NORFLEET Clk. Vestry

(46) January the 16/th/ 1765 Percessioned all the Lines between Abel MARTAIN and Esther pHELPS
The Lines between abel mARTAIN and Jemima mARTAIN
The Line between Demsey HINTON and Gabriel LACITER-
The Line between William HAYS and Gabriel LACITER
The Line between Gabriel LACITER and Maxeymillin mINSHARD (sic)
The Line between Gabriel LACITER and James BROWN-
The Line between Maxcyl? mINCHARD and John BROWN-
The Line betwen James bROWN and Maxeyn mINCHARD-
The Line betwen James bROWN and Jotham LACITER-
James bROWN and Richard mINeSHARD-

(46) (Cont.)
The Lines between James bROWN and Thomas hOULT-
The Line betwen Thomas HOLT and John LACITER-
The Line between John LACITER and mary aLPHIN
The Line between Mary aLPHIN and John SLAVIN-
The Line between John SLAVIN and Aaron BLANSHARD-
The Line between Aaron bLANSHARD and William BOND-
The Line between William bOND and micager BLANSHARD-
The Line between micager bLANSHARD and Timothy wALTON-
The Line between Micager and aron bLANSHARD
The Line between /A/aron bLANSHARD and Mary aLPHIN-
The Line between Aaron bLANSHARD and Richard mINCHEY
The Line between Richard mINCHEY and Jotham LACITER
The Line between Aaron Ser and Aaron bLANSHARD Junr-

(47) The Line between Richard mINCHEY and Josiah bLANSHARD
The Line between Josiah bLANSHARD and Jotham LACITER-
The Line between Jotham LACITER and Gabriel LACITER-
The Line between Gabriel LACITER and Josiah bLANSHARD
The Line between William bOND and ~~George~~ /Ozias/ LACITER
The Line between George LACITER and Ozias LACITER
The Line between Ozias LACITER and Robert LACITER
The Line between Robert LACITER and abisha LACITER
The Line between Robert LACITER and Demsey COSTEN-
The Line between Demsey COSTEN and William WALTON
The Line between William WALTON and Robert LACITER-
The Line between James COSTEN and william wALTON-
The Line between Richard bOND and James COSTEN
The Line between James COSTEN and william WALTON
The Line between William WALTON and Richard BOND
The Line between william wALTON william bOND-
The Line between William WALTON and Timothy wALTON-
The Line between Timothy wALTON and Micager BLANSHARD
The Line between William WALTON and palatiah wALTON
The Line between William WALTON and Thomas WALTON-
The Line between palatiah WALTON and Thomas wALTON-
The Line between Timothy wALTON and Robert HILL-
The Line between Robert HILL and Henry wALTON-
The Line between Henery wALTON and palatiah wALTON-
The Line between moses LACITER and James COSTEN Refused to be Perces/n?/ By? moses LACITER-

(48) In Obedience to an Order of Vestry Dated October the 23: 1764 We the Possessioners (sic) hath Processioned all the Land from Meherin Swamp up the Said Swamp to the Piping Branch So a Long the Sd. Branch to the Main Road and Down the Sd. Ro/a/d to Aron BLANSHARDs old Road and along the Sd. Old Road to BENNETs Creek Road up the Sd. Road to BENNETs Creek Bridg and then up BENNETs Creek to the Mill on Meharin Swamp

Palatiah WALTON
William bOND

(49) [No date] Agreable To anorder (sic) of vestery here unto Enext We The Subscribers have persesiond all The Lines In our Destrict Except one Lime Betwen Thomas hOSKENS and James pARKER the Sd hOSKENS Neglectd to Shaw the Line from The Indian Town Creek to Sandy Run and from Chowan River To the perquimon Road as witns our hands--

David WELCH

(49) (Cont.) William COPELAND

(50) In Obedience to an order of vestry Dated october 23/d/: 1764 we the processioners have processioned the Lines hereunder mentioned Vizt.

Lines Between Whom	Who present
John CRAVEN & Saml SWIFT	the parties
John CRAVEN & Wm. HARLOW	theparties
Saml SWIFT and Wm. HARLOW	the parties
Saml. SWIFT & Thos HUBBERT	the parties
Wm HARLOW & Rebecca GILBERT	theparties
Wm STEWART & Rebecca GILBERT	theparties
Abm. NORFLEET & Rebecca GILBERT	the parties
Abm. NORFLEET & Wm. STEWART	the parties
Wm S__WART & Sam/l/. SWIFT	one party and Phillip MCGUIRE
Abm. NORFLEET & Saml. MCGUIRE	the parties
Miles HALSEY & Saml. MCGUIRE	the parties
Miles HALSEY & Priscilla WOODARD under age	Miles HALSEY
Sam/l/. WOODARD & Rich/d/ WOODARD under age	Ann WOODARD
~~Sam/l/. WOODARD~~ & ~~Wm BOYD~~	
Sam/l/ WOODARD & Rich/d/. GLOHON	the parties
Wm BOYD & Rich/d/. GLOHON	Rich/d/ GLOHON
Wm. BOYD & Tho/s/ HOLLIDAY	the parties
Luke WHITE & Wm BOYD	Luke WHITE
Daniel EARL & Luke WHITE	the parties

Lines Between Whom	Who Present
Danel EARL & Peter pARKER	the parties
Wm BOYD & Peter PARKER	Peter PARKER
Wm. BOYD & Wm BOND	one party
Wm BOND & John BACCUS	the Parties
Wm BOYD & John BACCUS	one party

Peter PARKER
his
Samuel mCGUIER?
mark

(51) These Lines hereunder are unprocessioned for the Reasons as follows
John PAGET &}
John CRAVEN } CRAVEN Refusing
Tho/s/ HUBBERT &}
Saml SWIFT } SWIFTs Refuseing
Tho/s/ HUBBERT &}
Jessee BUNCH } BUNCH Refusing
Sarah LEWIS }

(51) (Cont.)
& Jessee BUNCH} Bounds uncertain
Shadrach BUNCH}
& Sarah LEWIS } neither of them appearing
John CAMPBELL }
& Shadrach BUNCH} CAMPBELL not in the Country
Wm BOYD and }
John CAMPBELL} CAMPBELL not in the Country
Wm BOYD & }
Sam/l/ W______} [Torn] BO__ _______g
John CAMPBELL}
& Sarah LEWIS} CAMPBELL Not in the Country

(52) North Carolina
Chowan County--ss-- Aprile Inferior Court
1765

Present His Majesties Justices
It was then & there ordered that Elisha HUNTER Esquire Surveyor of this County & William BOND, James BOND, Hance HOFFLER & abraham NORFLEET go round the lines of Mr. William BOYD's lands in this County between him & Samuell WOODWARD & that the said ffreeholders be sworn According to Law & that Elisha HUNTER Esqr. return the Same to next Court. Test Tho:JONES Cler:Cur

(53) [On back] Order to Procession the lines between Mr. Will/m/. BOYD & Samuell WOODWARD
Mr. BOYD refusing

The Within Order, Not Executed as it appeaed (sic) to be a mistake in the porsesioners Return the Line Refused to be porsesioned Was beteen Mr Wm. BOY (sic) & Richard MC GLOHAN as by? WOODWARD haveing Sold the S/d/ Land to MC GLOHAN Elisha HUNTER

(54) In Obedience to an order of Vestry Dated october 23/d/: 17654 We the Processioners Have Processioned Lines following Vizt.

Lines Between Whom	Who Present
Joseph ROGERS &	
Tho/s/ HOSKINS Junr	Joseph ROGERS
Joseph ROGERS &	
Charles ROBERTS	the Parties
Tho/s/ HOSKINS &	Wm ROBERTS
Charles ROBERTS	& Liles ROBERT
Charles ROBERTS &	
John PARRISH	the parties
David HUMPHRIES	
& John PARISH	the parties
Da_id HUMPHRYS	
& Charles ROBERTS	the Parties
David HUMPHRYS	
& Wm. HALSEY	the Parties
David HUMPHRYS	David HUM
& Wm ASHLEY	PHRYS (sic)
Wm ASHLY &	
John PARRISH	John PARISH
Lewis WARD &	

Lines Between Whom	Whom Present
Charles JORDAN Jun/r/	
& John JORDAN Junr	the Parties
Charles JORDAN Junr	
& Jacob ELLIS	the Parties
Charles JORDAN &	
Evan SKINNER	Charles JORDAN
Evan SKINNER &	
Jacob ELLIS	Jacob ELLIS
Evan SKINNER &	
Wm. SIMSONS	the Parties
Wm SIMSON &	
Jacob ELLIS	the Parties
Jacob ELLIS &	
John BRIN	the Parties
Jacob ELLIS &	
Ephraim ELLO?T	the parties
John JORDAN &	
John BRIN	John JORDAN
John BRIN	

(54) (Cont.)

Wm ASHLEY   Wm ASHLEY
Lewis WARD &
Wm MUNS   Wm MUNS
Tho/s/ MUNS &
Wm MUNS   the Parties
Tho/s/ MUNS &
Demsey BOND   Tho/s/ MUNS
under age
Sam/l/ HIX &   the Parties
Charles JORDAN Junr
Charles JORDAN Junr
& Wm MUNS   Wm MUNS
Charles JORDAN Sen/r/ the Parties
& Charles JORDAN Jun/r/
Charles JORDAN Senr
& John PARISH   John PARISH
Charles JORDAN Senr
& John JORDAN Junr John JORDAN

Francis SMITH   John BRIN
Hance HOFLER &   Hance HOFLER
Francis SMITH   & James HARRIS?
James HARRIS &
Francis SMITH   James HARIS
John BRIN &
John SIMSON   John BRIN
John BRIN &
Ephraim ELLOT   Ephraim ELLI_

(55) The Lines Between the persons Hereunder Named are unprocessioned for the following Reasons

Thomas HOSKINS Senr} HOSKINS Refusing
Wm BOND }
Tho/s/ HOSKINS Senr} HOSKINS Refusing
James BOND }
Tho/s/ HOSKINS Senr} HOSKINS Refusing
Hances HOFLER }
Tho/s/ HOSKINS} HOSKINS Refusing
John PARISH }
Tho/s/ HOSKINS Senr} HOSKINS Refusing
Wm HALSEY }
Tho/s/ HOSKINS Senr} HOSKINGS Refusing
Lewis JORDAN }
Tho/s/ HOSKINS Senr} HOSKINS Refusing
Wm ASHLEY }
Patrick HIX } HIX Refusing
Wm. COTTERAL}
Joshua DEAL} DEAL Refusing
Mary SIMSON}
Tho/s/ STREATOR } STREATOR Sick
Charles ROBERT } not able to appear
Tho/s/ LUTEN Senr} LUTEN Not able
Tho/s/ MCWIDER } to Go

Joseph PARRISH
his
Tho/s/ 7 BACCUS   Processioners
mark

(56) North Carolina
Chowan County ss--Aprill Inferior Court 1765.
Present His Majesties Justices
It was then and there Ordered that Elisha HUNTER Esquire Surveyor of this County and

(56) (Cont.) Messrs. Evan SKINNER, William COTTERELL, Charles JORDAN Senior, & Thomas MC NIDER do Proceed by the lines running between Thomas HOSKINS Senior and ~~John PARISH~~ /William HALSEY/ and that the said ffreeholders be sworn According to Law and that Elisha HUNTER Esquire return the same to Next Court.

Test Tho:JONES. Cler:Cur.

(57) [On back] Order to Procession between Thomas HOSKINS Senior & Will/m/. HALSEY--

Thomas HOSKINS the Party refusing

(58) North Carolina}
Chowan County } In Obeadiance to Several Orders of the C? Infearior Court of S/d/. Coun/ty/ Ordering Mess/rs/. Evan SKINNER Wm. COTTRELL ~~John~~ Charles JORDAN & Thos MC. NIDER to go on the Lines between Thos. HOSKINS & Wm. HALSEY Which we haveing Done in the following manner. begining at a Gum Standing on the No Side of the Branch known by Name of Spring Branch & on the West Side of aSmall Branch that Issueth out of Sd. branch Runing then With Sd. its (sic) Several Courses to John ROBENSONs Corner pine then on ROBENSONs Line it appearing to us to be the Devideing line betwen /Sd. HOSKINS &/ Elender ASHLEY to Lewis JORDANs line then on the line betwee/n/ ~~Th~~ S/d/. HOSKINS and S/d/. JORDAN on the Oald bounded line of marked trees Which appeard. to be the Deviding Line of S/d/. Lands to his Corner ---
Then on the lands between S/d/. HOSKINS and John PARISH by a New line of marked trees == as No Oald ones Was to be found agreed on by the parties begining Near a Pososon Caled the Woolf Den & and Runing through S/d/. Wolf Den No 80/d/ West to a ~~f~~ Red Oak Standing in a flat Branch then along S/d/. Branch by a line of marked trees So 60/d/ W to the the (sic) Center of Three large pines then S/o/. 40 Wt along S/d/. Branch to John WATSONs Line then on S/d/. WATSONs line No 50 d Wt to his Corner-----
Then on the lines between S/d/. HOSKINS and Hance HOFFLER S/o/. 55 Wt 132 pole-----
Then on the lines between S/d/. HOSKINS & Wm. BOND begining at a marked White Oak Standing on the S/o/ Side of Deep Run Runing then So 34 d Wt 40 pole to a Smal Red Oak then S/o/ 70 Et to a Corner pine then by the Oald bounded line to a Small Branch then up Sd Branch to a White Oak then on the pat

(59) tent line to the Senter of five pines Standing in a branch that Issueth outt of Deep Run then Down S/d/ Run to the first Station the afore S/d/. lines all Renewed July ye 9th 10th 12th 1765 the afore S/d/. Freeholders Was first Sworn according to Law------

July ye 17 1765 then Messrs. William BOND James BOND Hance HOFFLER & Abraham NORFLEET went on the Lines between Wm. COTTRELL & Patrick HICK (sic) and Renewed the Oald lines Which appeard to us to be the Bounds between S/d/. COTTREEL & S/d/ HICKS they being first Duly Sworn according to law---

July ye 11/th/ 1765 Messrs Thos. HOSKINS John HOSKI/NS/ John PARISH & Thos. BACKERS Went on the Lines between Mary SIMSON & Joshua DEAL and Renewd the Oald bounded lines as appeard to us to be the bounds between S/d/. SIMSON & S/d/. DEAL they being first Sworn according to Law Certified pr

Elisha HUNTER

(60) [On back] Mr. HUNTERs return's concerning Processioners Returns

[NOTE: The following appears parallel to the right edge of this sheet.]

~~Isaac~~ /Willm./ HARRELL his will aprill 1762
[At bottom of page.] 3?76

(61) North Carolina
Chowan County ss
To the Worshipfull Justices of Chowan County Inferior Court &t the Petition of John LEWIS Junior Humbly sheweth that your Petitioner was Appointed with Josiah SMALL by the vestry of the parish of Saint Paul to Procession certain Lands &t within the County aforesaid your Petitioner what with the very wet weather in the winter & his crop coming on after Aprill Court last had it not in his power to Comply with the said order of Court /vestry/ your petitioner therefore most humbly prays your worships to grant him the Continuance of the said order untill the next Inferior Court in October as by that time he

(62) will have complied with the said order & your Petitioner in duty bound will ever pray &t. John LEWIS Junior
July 22/d/ 1765

(63) [On back] John LEWIS Junior his Petition as one of the Processioners----

Chowan County Processioners' Record, 1756, 1795-1808, 2 vols. C.024.48006

Years: 1795-1808 Pages: 1-13

(64) [1] [Margin: No 1] State of North Carolina }
Chowan County Decr. 8/th. 1795} Survayed and processioned for Charles HAUGHTON as follows Viz: begining at a persimmon R. MINGs Jessee HASSELLs & the Said HAUGHTONs Corner & Runing South Sixty nine west one hundred &fifty five poles to the Said C. HAUGHTONs Road then up the Said Road North Sixty one West-Ninty two poles, the (sic) north forty five East Ninty poles to a Black gum, then north thirty three west thirty nine Poles to the main Road then up the road South fifty Eight west Eighty nine Poles. then South thirty five West thirty Eight poles then South Sixty three West Twenty two poles. then South forty five west forty-four poles then South Seventy west Seventy poles-to a Center Persimmon white Oak & WmGREGORYs Corner Then up his line South thirty Seven East (sic) to a Center ash &maple Then South thirteen west twenty one poles to a Maple--Edward HAUGHTONs J BLOUNTs dec/d/. Corner then north Seventy Nine East ninty Poles to Holly Oak & ash, then North Seventy Seven East One hundred & thirteen Poles to two Hollys Beach & Gum then South Seventy east one hundred & Twenty two poles to Chinquipin Persimmon & Gum Then North Eleven east ninty Six poles to Ash Gum & two Pines Thomas REAs & John NORCOMs Corner, then North three west One hundred and twenty poles to REAs lane then North twenty two west one hundred and nine poles a persimmon Richard MINGs &Said HAUGHTONs Corner then Binding on MINGs to the first Station. Surveyed and Processioned for Seven hundred and thirteen Acres of Land by me
----
713 Acres
Returned according to Law} Signed George BAINS Senr. Pr.
Test ENORFLEET Cll

(65) [2] [Margin: No 2] State of North Carolina}
Chowan County } September Term 1796
Survayed for George BAINES Senior William BAINS Junr. & George BAINS the younger Viz: This Plan represents the

(65) (Cont.) land in possession of George BAINS Senr. William BAINS &George BAINS the younger Lying in Chowan County, Butted and Bounded as folloeth, Begining at a Cypruss in yeopim River Swamp Doctr. Samuel DICKINSONs line, & the County line, then runing South 42 1/2 Wt. 246. poles Binding Thomas WARDs patant Line to a Bunch of Gums then Binding TRULOVEs patantline So. 16 Et. 48 poles to water Oak Jacob BLOUNTs George BAINS Junr. & Thomas WARDs Corner then with George BAINS Junr. Patant So 70 Wt. 79 Poles to a Gum & ash then No. 26 Wt. 32 Chain to a poplar then So. 45 Wt. 95 poles to Henderson STANDINs line thence with his No. 64. Wt. 208 poles to a white Oak then No. 9 Wt 9 Poles to a pine Stump--then No. 27. Wt. 47 poles to apine by the Ponds, old field then with George BAINS Junrs. line No 17 Chains to a Gum then then (sic) no. 60 Wt. 52 Chain to apine & two Gums in Lemuel STANDINs line by his fence then with his line No 5. Chain to two Sassafrases then No 40. Wt. 120 poles to aGum then Then (sic) No 49 Wt. 96 pole to a pine Joshua JOHNSON & James JONES's Corner then with JONES's line No:11 Wt. 7 Poles to Michal MCKEELs Corner water Oaks, then with his line No. 7 1/2 Chain to a Gum & Maple then No 45. Et. 58 Chain to A Dead pine Saplin Capt. John NORCOMs Corner tree, then with his line So 88. Et. 88. Chain to a pine in Job BRANCHes line, then with his line So 18 Wt. 20 Chain to a pine then So 5 1/4 Chain to a Gum Sd. BRANCHes, & Delight NIXSONs Corner tree then with NIXONs line So. 3 1/2 Chain to William LITTLEJOHNs line a Pine, then with his line No 78 Wt. 32 Chain to a pine then South 36 Wt. 10 Chain to a pine then So 7 Wt.

(66) [3] 13 Chain to a pine then So: /50/ Et. 23 Chain to apine on the South East of the Oak Lands then So. 85. Et. 20 1/2 Chain to a forked pine then So 68 Et. 28 Chain to apine, then Leaving LITTLEJOHNs line So. 14 Chain to aGum & Oak Thomas KINGsJunr Corner then with his line So 35 Et. 17 Chain to a Cypress in the Aforesaid Swamp then down the run of the Swamp the Various Courses there of to the first Station Containing 1675 Acres Surveyed June the 6/th/. 7/th/. 8/th/ and September the 9/th/. and 10/th/ 1796.

In Obedience to the Order of Court hereunto returned I have processioned the Lines of the lands of George BAINS Sene?r. &c &cc as above Stated, Present Jacob BLOUNT Esqr. George BAINS Junr. &Lemuel STANDIN, When on their lines.

Acres Land
1675 (Signed) JoRIDDICK
Test ENORFLEET C11

(67) [4] [Margin: No3] State of North Carolina} Surveyed & processioned on the Chowan County } 5/th/. 6.7/th/ & 8/th/. December 1796 & on the 16/th/ & 23/d/. of January 1797. for William BENNETT as followas. Vizt. begining at Rockahock Creek at the Side of the Said Creek at Stephen ELIOTTs Corner and runing Along ELLOTTs (sic) line N. 89. E 170. poles to the path then S. 78. E 110 poles to a pine HINSLEYs ~~line~~ Corner by the road then along his line S. 50 E. 106. poles to a Sweet gum his Corner in Micajah BUNCHes line then along BUNCHes line N 32 E 85 poles to a popler &Gum, then S 34 E. 90 poles - to two white Oakes and aGum then N. 30 E 65. poles to A Center of 3 dog woods and a pine BUNCHes and Colo. John BONDs Corner Then along BONDs line No 50. W. 120. poles to a Maple Then N 25. E 102. poles to a pine Then N 41 W. 44 poles to aBlack Gum Then N55. E 65 poles to a Sweet Gum in BONDs line Then N55. W. 100 poles to a White Oake Nicholas NEWBORNs and LAWRENCEs Corner -- Then S 71. W. 80. poles to NEWBORNs and John COFFIELDs Corner Apine By the Road Then along COFFIELDs line N 69 W 124 poles to the Mill pond Then up the Mill pond to the Mouth of a Branch Near pARKERs Landing, or the landing By PARKERs then up the Said Reedy Branch the Various Courses there of to a poplar and Gum Then S. 40. W. 142 poles to an old Pine AMBROS's Corner, Now Nathanl. BRINs Then along BRINS and Abraham NORFLEETs line N 38. W. 418. poles to 3 water θ Gums in the Juniper pocosin Then S. 42. W. 86 poles to two white Bays & a maple and Then William LEWIS's line N. 53 1/2 W. 89 poles to two pines and an Oak James GORDONs Corner Then along his line S. 2 1/2. E. 275. poles to apine a

(67) (Cont.) Corner of John PADJETTs (sic) and Mrs. Mary MCGUIREs Then along Mrs. MCGEUIREs line S. 3 E 147 poles to apine Then S. 88. W 355 poles to Chowan River Then Dawn the River S 45. E 200 poles to HARRISes landing and Still

(68) [5] Still Dawn the River and up the Bay the Various Courses - there of to the Mouth of Rockahock Creek, Then Runing up the Chanel of the Creek on the S. East Side of aLittle Island Including it on William BENNETTs Side of the Said Channel and Still along the Channel of the Creek to the first Station, Containing Four Thousand Seven hundred Acres --
Surveyed and processioned the 5/th/. 6. 7. 8/th/. of December 1796 and on the 16th. & 23/d/. of January 1797. Present when on their lines, John BOND, Nicholas NEWBORN, John COFFIELD. Abraham NORFLEET, Nathaniel BRINN James GORDON John PADJETT Joseph HINSLEY and Micajah BUNCH, (blank) MCGEI?YER in behalf of Mary MCGEW?IRE, & Phillip MCGWIRE on Behalf of Elizabeth ELLIOTT widow of Stephen ELIOTT decsd.
4700 acres Land (Signed) (blank)
Test George BAINS Process/r/:/C?C?
ENORFLEET C11

(69) [6] [Margin: No4] State of North Carolina}
Chowan County } Surveyed, & processioned for Fredrick CREECY the twenty Second day of May 1797-- Begining at aSmall Sweet Gum near Jessee HASSELLs bars, (sic) runing north five degrees West Eighty five poles to a Gum Stump & persimmon, Jonathan HAUGHTONs Corner Still -- Binding on HAUGHTONs line North Seventy Seven West Sixty One poles to the main Road then up the Road South Thirty five west, Eighty two poles to a Small Branch, then down Said Branch to the old road South forty five - East thirteen poles, then South fifty five West thirty four Poles to two red Oakes and a pine Stump -- Thomas MINGs and Charles HAUGHTONs Corner, then aLong HAUGHTONs Line South thirty five East, thirty two Poles to a Gum Charles HAUGHTONs and Jesse HASSELs -- Corner then aLong HASSELLs line North Sixty one degrees East Sixty four poles to a pine and then Still along his line South Forty five East forty poles to a Sweet Gum, then Still on his line by the line of marked trees to the first Station Containing Sixty one acres.

Also an Other Tract of Land, Containing two hundred and fifteen acres beging (sic) at two Red Oakes & apine Stump MINGs & HAUGHTONs Corner then along HAUGHTONs line South forty five west Eighty Poles, to an Oak, then Still along HAUGHTONs Line North Sixty four west one hundred and Sixty Six poles to a Center of two water Oakes and aGum and Holly HAUGHTONs and Jacob BLOUNTs Corner Then Binding on BLOUNTs, North twelve west Ninty two poles to a Center, Gum white Oak, Hickory and pine So Still on BLOUNTs line North twenty East one hundred and Seventy four Poles to BLOUNTs Canel Ditch, Then

(70) [7] Then Dawn Said Ditch South Seventy two East Ninety Eight Poles to a Center of two Gums and two Hollys on MINGs line then along MINGs line South Eighteen West one hundred and fifty eight poles into the Ridge Plantation Then Still on MINGs line South fifty Six East fifty One poles to a Dead popler then South forty East - Thirteen poles then South forty five East Eighteen Poles then Still on MINGs line by the Marked Trees to the first Station
61. acres (Signed) George BAINS Processioner
213 of C. County.
276 acres
Test ENORFLEET C11
Present when on their lines, Jesse HASSEL, Jonathan HAUGHTEN Jacob BLOUNTs Overseer. (Samuel REA) Delilah MING gave me her papers and Consented, Charles HAUGHTON like wise Give (sic) his Consent
(Signed) George BAINS P. C. C

(71) [8] [Margin: No 5] State of North Carolina}
Chowan County } Surveyed and processioned for Mr. Edward McGuyer WOOD WARD (sic) a Certain Tract or parcel of Land lying in Chowan County in the fork of Rockahock Swamp where on the Said WOOD WARD now lives--Begining at aBlack Gum a Corner of Julius BUNCHes des/d/. John COFFIELDs and WOOD WARDs then binding on Said COFFIELDs line- A Cross the Ridge No 39. E. 84 poles to a Cypress in a B. Branch (sic) a Corner of Said COFFIELDs in - Charles JOHNSONs line, then Binding on Said JOHNSONs line along the run of Said Branch to a Cypress in the Swamp by the Side of a Ditch then down Said JOHNSONs ditch to aBridge, then Still down the run of the Swamp by Various Courses, binding on BUNCHes Land to the first Station Containing Sixty two Acres --

Surveyed & processioned the 1/st/ day of November 1797. Present on their lines John COFFIELD, Charles JOHNSON & Soloman BUNCH Son of Said Julius BUNCH 62 Acres
George BAINS Senr. Pro
Test ENORFLEET Cll

(72) [9] State of North Carolina}
Chowan County ......} Joseph REDDICK being appointed Processioner to Procession the Lands of George BAINES Senr. William BAINS & George BAINS Junr. .. reports Vizt Persuent (sic) to Order of the Court of Chowan I proceeded to-Procession the lines of the Lands of George BAINS Senr. &cc as dirited pr. Said Order, after Proceeding Some distance on the Lines of Said BAINS &c without interruption we arriv/d/ to the Lines that Devided the Lands of the Said George BAINS &c and the Lands of Lemuel STANDIN, Michael MCKEEL & forbid me of Proceding any further on the Business of Processioning the Lines of the Land of the Said BAINS &c Saying that he claimed aright to apart of the Land within the Bounds that the Sd.. BAINS &c Claimed The Bound of which he Cannot Clarely (sic) assertain, -- But that he hath apatent for the Same, in Cases of this Kind the Act of Assembly hath proveded, and Directed the Method to be persued which I make no Doubt the Court will proceed to do the above is a True State of the Case Certified under my hand &seal 10th day of April 1800

To the worshipful Court} JoRIDDICK (Seal)
of the County of Chowan}
State of North Carolina} Chowan County Court
June Term 1800
George BAINS & others}
vs } Disputed Line between the
Michal MCKEELL } Parties on Processioning as pr the above Report, Ordered that Baker HOSKINS Benjamin COFFIELD Edward HAUGHTON, Arthur HOWE and

(73) [10] and Richard HAUGHTON free holders be Appointed to Proceed with the Processioner on the Line or Lines So disputed and Procession the Same and make report of their proceedings to the next Term Agreeable to the Directions of the Act of Assembly By order
Test ENORFLEET Cll

In Obedience to the Order of Court hereunto annexed We Richard HAUGHTON, Arthur HOWE Edward HAUGHTON and Baker HOSKINS being appointed by Court &Lemuel STANDIN being Chosen by George BAINS & Michal MCKEELL in Place of Benjamin COFFIELD who was one appointed by Court - being Sick & not able to attend have met on the disputed Lines of the Said George BAINS & Michal MCKEELL, and find that the Patents of George BAINS are of older date than the Patents of Michal MC.KEELL and it appearing there was vacant Land joining the Said George BAINSs Patent - where on the Said Michal MCKEELL might have laid his Survey without laying it within the lines of the Said George BAINS & no other Legal Claim except that - of Senior Entrys, and for the Causes Aforesaid we are

(73) (Cont.) of the Opinion that the Senior patent have its Course Agreeable to the Plat here unto annexed which appears to be the Lines &Bounds of the Said Patents --

Given under Our hands this 4/th/ day of August 1800,

Richard HAUGHTON
Arthur HOWE
JoREDDICK Pror. Edwd. HAUGHTON
Baker HOSKINS
LemlSTANDIN

This Plan (sic)

(74) [11] [Margin: No. 6.-1673 Acres] This Plan represents the Land in Possession of George BAINS Senr. William BAINS & George BAINS Junr. lying in Chowan County -- Beginning at a pine Stump on the Swamp of yeopim River James MINGs Corner thence So. 42 1/2 Wt. 226 pole. Binding - Thomas WARDs patent line, to aBunch of Gums then Binding TRULOVEs patent line So 16 Et 48 pole to a water Oak Jacob BLOUNTs and Said George BAINSs Corner Tree then So 70. Wt 79 pole to a Gum & Ash No. 26. Wt 35. Ch: to apoplar So. 45 wt 95 pole to Henderson STANDINs line, then with his line No. 64 Wt 208 pole to a white Oak No. 9. Wt. 9 pole to a pine Stump - No. 27. Wt 47 pole to a pine by the Ponds old field, then with George BAINES decased line No 17. Chains to aGum No 60 Wt. 52 Chains to a pine & two Gums in Lemuel STANDINs Line by his Fence Then with his line No 5. Ch: to two Sassafrases, No 40. Wt 120 Poles to aGum No 49. Wt 96. Poles to apine Joshua JOHNSONs and James JONES.s Corner Tree, then with JONES.s line No. 11. Wt 7 Pole to Michal MCKEELs Corner, water Oak No 7 1/2 Chain to aGum& maple No 45. Et 58. Ch: to aDead pine Saplin -- Capt. John NORCOMs Corner Tree, then with his line So 88. Et 38. Chain to four Pines in Job BRANCHes line then with his line So. 18. Wt. 20 Ch. to apine So 5 1/4 Ch. to aGum Sd. BRANCHes and Deleight NICKSONs Corner Tree then with NICKSONs line So. 3 1/2 Ch: to William LITTLEJOHNs Esqrs. line then with his line No. 78 Wt 32 Ch: to apine So 36 Wt 10. Ch: to apine, So 7. Wt. 13 Ch: to a pine So 50. Et 23 Ch: to apine on the South Edge of the Oak land, So 85 - Et 20 1/2 Ch: to aforked pine, So 68. Et 28. Ch to apine then leaving LITTLEJOHNs line So. 14 Ch: to aGum & Oak Thomas MINGs Corner Tree, then with his line So 35 Et 17 Ch: to a Cypriss in the aforesaid yeopim River Swamp then down the run of the Said Swamp the various Courses thereof, untill it Comes opperset (sic) the first Station then to the first Station Containing Sixteen hundred & Seventy three Acres
N.B the lines marked-a.b.c.d. & E. are the lines disputed by M. MCKEEL,
& processioned for Geo: BAINS. Jo REDDICK processioner
Augt 1800 --

(75) [12] State of North Carolina March Term 1808
Chowan County } James BAINS County -- Processioner, having reported to the Court, that he was forbid Running the line between Jesse HASSELL & Charles HAUGHTON by Said Charles

Ordered that Fredrick LUTEN, Thomas MIERS George BAINS, Job PETTIJOHN & Fredrick CREECY - be appointed to attend with the processioner on the Lines in dispute and proceed to Establish Such disputed line or lines as Shall appear tothem Right, and procession the Same and make report of their proceedings to next Term

by Order
Test ENORFLEET Cl

June Term 1808. the Order renewed

In Obedience the Order (sic) of Court we the Subscribers have met on the Premisas as Directed and on examining the Lines in dispute, we have Desided in favour of the Claims of Jessee HASSELL in the Following Manner - Begining at Charles HAUGHTONs Road in the Dividing line Between Jesse HASSELL & Charles HAUGHTON - running thence along S/d/. dividing line from Said Road S. 68. W. 76. poles to aMaple Stand at the Edge of the percose?rn then along the Said Percorsen (sic) N. 3 W. 67. poles to a Centre of

(75) (Cont.) three trees a Dead pine, Gum & Maple Standing on Said Charles HAUGHTONs Road it including the peace (sic) of Land in dispute Between Said Road & the percorsen Containing Fourteen Acres that Was in dispute which will more fully appear by having refference to the Platt of the Said

(76) [13] [Margin: No. 7. 155. Acres] Land that here with appears. Given under our hands this 7/th/ day ofSeptemtemter (sic) 1808.

Job PETTIJOHN
FredLUTEN
Thomas MING
Fredrick CREECY
George BAINS

The above Plott represents a Tract of Land Surveyed and processioned for Jesse HASSELL, Begining at the run of Creek Fork at the Foot of a lain Running up Said Lain S. 68. W. 232. poles to a Maple. then N. 3. W. 67. Poles to a Centre of three trees Pine Gum & maple. then N. 45. E. 90 poles to Centre of 4 trees N. 55. E. 63. poles to Pine then S. 46. E. 41. poles to aGum then No. 64 E. 33. poles to a Gum N/th/. 6. W 47. poles. to apine at the Corner of John HAUGHTONs Land then N. 84. E. 84 poles to the run ofCreek Fork then up the Various Corses (sic) to an ash then S. 14. W. 21 Poles to an ash at the run of Said Creek Fork then up The Various Corses of the Same to the first Station. It Being the foot of the Dividing line Between Jessee HASSELL & Charles HAUGHTON Surveyed and Plotted September 7/th/ 1808.

James BAINES C Pr.

Thomas MIERS
Charlto MIRES} Chain Barers

[Note: No graphic plats are found in this book.]

END OF BOOK

APPENDIX A

The following orders for processioning are taken from Vestry Minutes of St. Paul's Parish, Chowan County, North Carolina 1701-1776[1]

(77a) p. 126 "At a Vestry Met and Held at Constants Chappel on satterday The 25th Day of October Anno Dom 1755. . . .

The Vestry Takeing into consideration The Law for Settleing the Title and Bounds of Peoples Lands, by freeholders appointed To Procession The Same On Oath &c. Accordingly Proceed to Divide The Parish into Convenient Cantons and to Appoint Two Freeholders in Each Canton Processioners to procession The same according To Law, as Follows.

Ordered That Francis SANDERS and John MINSHEE do Procession all The Lands from Abraham ODAMs as The Road Runs to Mehe____ Ferrey which is bounded between The Road and The River.

Ordered That Edward HAIR Juner and Joseph SPEIGHT Do Procession all The Lands from the Road that Leads by Abraham ODAMs to Meherin Ferrey begining at the Cuntry Line so along Sarum Road To PUGHs Road and so a Long that Road to the Ferrey.

Ordered That Jacob ODAM and James BRADDY do procession All the Lands from PUGHes Road, beginning at the Plantation of Robert RODGERS so a long Sarum Road to the Notty Pine Swamp down the Said Swamp to Henry BAKERs Mill so along The Road That Leads by William UMPHLETs to PUGHs Road."

(78a) p. 127 "Ordered That Jethro HARRIL and John SKINNER Procession All The Lands from Henry BAKERs Mill begining at the Mill down Coles Creek to the River, up The River to Cottons Ferrey, then a Long the Road to Henry BAKERs Mill.

Ordered That Robert RODGERS and John ARLINE do Procession all The Lands from The Cuntry Line begining near Moses PARKER (?) on The New Road ____ ____ The Said Road to The Road (?) at (91) ____ ____ Sarum Road to The Cuntry ____.

Ordered That William POWELL Juner. and Richard FELTON Senior Procession all The Lands from the New Road begining at The head of Bennets Creek down The said Creek To the Mouth of The Honeypot Swamp, up the said Swamp to The head of it, & so a Cross to the head of The Knotty Pine Swamp and down The said swamp To The New Road.

Ordered That William DANIEL and James PILAND do Procession All The Lands from The new Road begining where The new Road crosses The Notty Pine Swamp, Thence up the said swamp to the head there of Then a cross from That to the Honey pot Swamp and then down the Same to Bennets Creek & Down the said Creek to The River thence up the River to Coles Creek and up the said Creek to the Notty Pine Swamp and up the Swamp to The New Road.

Ordered That William POWELL senior and Edward ARNELL Procession all The Lands

(78a) (Cont.) from The Head of Bennetts Creek begining at the Cuntry Line up Chowan Road to The Loosing Swamp & up the said Swamp by The flat Branch across to Bennets Creek and up the said Bennets Creek to The Cuntry Line and a Long the Line to Chowan Road.

Ordered That Samuel HARRILL and John RICE Procession all The Lands from The Loosing Swamp down Perquimons Road to SPEIGHTs Plantation Thence by the Cart Road That Leads to Elisha HUNTERs, Then down by Meherrin Swamp to Bennets Creek and up the Creek to The Flat Branch then by the Loosing Swamp to Perquimons Road.

Ordered That Robert LASITER and Moses LASITER Procession all The Lands Included from Meherrin Swamp begining at Jacob HUNTERs Mill up the Said Swamp to The piping Branch so along The said branch to The Main Road and Down The said Road to Aaron BLANSHARDs Old Road and a Long the Said old Road To Bennets Creek road up the said Road to Bennets Creek Bridg_ and thence up Bennets Creek To the Mill on Meherrin Swamp.

Ordered That Jesse HUNTER and Benjamin BLANSHARD do Procession all The Lands included from Bennets Creek Road Begining at Bennets Creek Bridge ___ ___ ___ Creek Road Catherins Creek Bridge Down Catharins Creek to The River, up The River to The Mouth of Bennets Creek and up Bennets Creek to Bennets Creek Bridge.

Ordered That Abner EASON and Guy HILL do Procession all The Lands Included Begining at SPEIGHTses Plantation So along the Road to James SCOTTs, Thence Down Catharin Creek to The Road at Thomas WALTONs, Thence along Bennets Creek Road to BLANSHARDs Old Road so

(79a) p. 128 along the said Road to Chowan Road & so to The Piping Branch then down ye Branch to meherin Swamp and down ye Swamp to Elisha HUNTERs and from thence by his Cart Road to SPEIGHTes Plantation.

Ordered That James SUMNER and Richard FREEMAN Procession All The Lands included Between Catharins Creek, The Sandy Run and Perquimons Road - begining at James SCOTs Plantation.

Ordered That William COUPLAND and Nathan PARKER do Procession all The Lands included between The Sandy Run and Indian Town Creek, Chowan River and Perquimons.

Ordered That William BOYD and Luke White do Procession All the Lands Included between Indian Town Creek and Rockahock Creek between the Main Road and Chowan River and make Return Thereof To April Court.

Ordered That William BOND and Charles ROBERTS do Procession all The Lands Included between Indian Town Creek and Machacoma Creek alis. Garbacon between the main Road and Perquimons County and make Return thereof to Aprill County Court.

Ordered That William LUTEN and William WESTEN do Procession all The Lands That are Included between Rocahock and Machacoma Creek on the West side of the Main Road between The Road and Chowan River and That They make Return There of to April Court next.

Ordered That Thomas BONNER and Nathaniel HOCOTT do Procession all The Lands That are Included between Machacoma Creek alis Garbac__ and William ____ ____ ____ to the River &c. (92)

(79a) (Cont.) _______ ____ _ohn BENBURY and Robert BEASLEY __ Procession all The Lands That are Included between William HORSKINSes Mill Swamp The Sound side and Yeopim River and make Return Thereof To April Court Next according To Law."

(80a) p. 158 "At a Vestry met at the Church in Edenton Tuesday the 23d Day of October 1764. . . .

The Vestry Taking into Consideration the Law for Settleing the Title and Bounds of Peoples Lands By Freeholders appointed to procession the Same on oath &c. Accordingly proceed to Divide the Parish into Convenient Cantons and to appoint Two freeholders in Each Canton processioners to procession the Same according to Law as follows.

Ordered that David JONES and Jacob NORFLEET procession all the Lands from the Head of Bennets Creek Begining at the Country Line up Chowan road to the Loosing Swamp and up the Said Swamp By the flat Branch across to Bennets Creek and up the Said Bennets Creek to the Country Line and a Long the Line to Chowan Road and make return Thereof to April Court next according to Law.

Ordered That Isaac HARREL and David RICE Procession all the Lands from the Loosing Swamp Down Perquimons road to SPEIGHTs Plantation thence by the Cart road that Leads to Elisha HUNTERs then Down By Meherin Swamp to Bennets Creek and up the Creek to the Flat Branch then By the Loosing Swamp to perquimons road and make return to april Court Next according to Law.

Ordered That William BOND and Palatiah WALTON procession all the Lands included from Meherin Swamp Begining at Jacob HUNTERs

(81a) p. 159 Mill up the Said Swamp to the Pipeing Branch so along the said Branch to the main road and Down the Said Road to Aaron BLANSHARDs old Road and long the Said old Road To Bennets Creek Road up the Said road to Bennets Creek Bridge and thence up Bennets Creek to the Mill on Meherin Swamp and make Return to April Court Next according to Law.

Ordered That William FREEMAN Junr. And Jonas HINTON Do procession all the Lands included From Bennets Creek road Begining at Bennets Creek Bridge Down Bennets Creek road to Catherines Creek Bridge Down Catherins Creek to the River up the River to the mouth of Bennets Creek and up Bennets Creek to Bennets Creek Bridge and make return to April Court Next according to Law.

Ordered That Amos TROTMAN and Micajah HILL Do procession all the Lands included Begining at SPEIGHTs Plantation So along the Road to The Widow SCOTs Thence Down Catherins Creek to the Road at Richard WALTONs Then Along Bennets Creek Road to BLANCHARDs old Road so along The Said Road To Chowan Road and so to the piping Branch Then Down the Branch to Meherin Swamp and Down The Swamp to Elisha HUNTERs and from Thence By his Cart Road to SPEIGHTs Plantation and make Return to April Court Next according to Law.

Ordered That Charls ROUNTRY and John WALLIS do procession all the Lands included Betwen Catherins Creek The Sandy Run and perquimons Road Begining at The Widow SCOTs Plantation and make Return to April Court Next according to Law.

Ordered That David WELSH and William COUPLAND Do Procession all the Lands included Between the Sandy Run and Indian Town Creek Chowan River and perquimons And make Return to April Court Next according To Law.

(81a) (Cont.) Ordered That Peter PARKER and Samuel MCGUIRE Do Procession all the Lands included Between Indian Town Creek and Rockahock Creek Between the Main Road and Chowan River and make Return Thereof To April Court Next according To Law.

Ordered That William WESTON and Thomas MCNIDER Do procession all the Lands That are included Between Rockahock Creek and Machacoma Creek on the West Side of the main Road between the Road & Chowan River. (117)

Ordered That Thomas BONNER Senr. And Richard HOSKINS do procession all the Lands that are included Between Machacoma Creek and William HOSKINS's Mill Swamp to the River and make Return Thereof to April Court Next according to Law.

Ordered That Thomas HOSKINS and James BLOUNT Do procession all the Lands that are included between William HOSKINS Mill Swamp the Sound Side and yeopim River and make Return thereof To April Court Next according to Law.

Ordered That Thomas BACCUS and Joseph PARISH Do procession all the Lands that are included Between the Main road and Sandy

(82a) p. 160 ridge road up to Indian Town Creek and make Return thereof To April Court Next according to Law.

Ordered That Evan SKINNER and William ASHLEY Do Procession all the Lands That are included Between Sandy Ridge Road and the perquimon line up to the Widow ASHLEYs Thence along the Cart road to Little PARKERs and make Return thereof to april Court Next according To Law.

Ordered That John LEWIS Junr. and Josiah SMALL Do procession all the Lands that are included Between The Main Road perquimons Line Machacoma Creek And the Cart way from the Widow ASHLEYs to Little PARKERs and make Return thereof to April Court Next according to Law."

* * * * *

[1]Fouts, Raymond Parker, Vestry Minutes of St. Paul's Parish, Chowan County, North Carolina 1701-1776 (Cocoa, FL: GenRec Books, 1983)

APPENDIX B

The following are reduced copies of the original documents as found in the North Carolina State Archives. The negative pages are from microfilm.

The numbers on the upper right side of these pages correspond with the assigned numbers in the text for convenient reference.

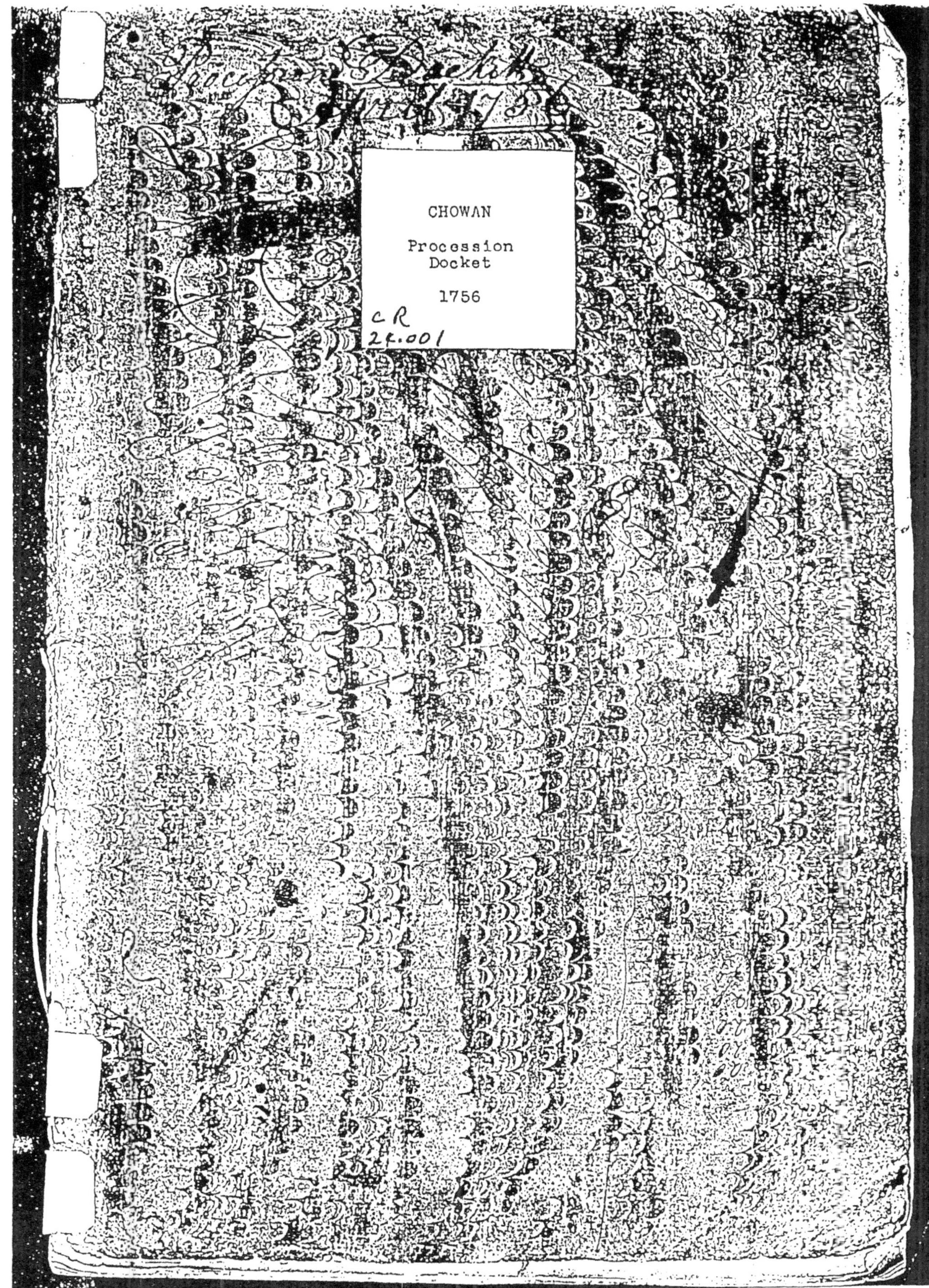
CHOWAN
Procession
Docket
1756
CR
24.001

(1)

Processioned the Line between John Hittrel and William Waters both parties present likewise Daniel Pugh and Richard Baker.

Processioned the Line between Richard Baker and John Hittrel both Parties present likewise Daniel Pugh and Stephen Parker

Processioned the Line between William Waters and Richard Baker both parties present likewise Daniel Pugh and Thomas Baker.

Processioned the Line between William Waters and Richard Parker both Parties present, likewise Daniel Pugh and Jacob Boyjus.

Processioned the Line between Richard Baker and Richard Parker both parties present likewise Daniel Pugh and Thomas Wiggins.

Processioned the Line between Epaphroditus Boyce and Richard Baker both parties present, likewise Daniel Pugh and Thomas Wiggons

Processioned the Line between Richard Barker and Ephphraditus Boyce both parties present likewise Daniel Pugh and Thomas Wiggons

Processioned the Line between Daniel Pugh and Epaphraditus Boyce both parties present likewise Richard Baker and Thomas Wiggons

Processioned the Line between Daniel Pugh and Richard Brothers both Parties present Thomas Wiggons & Micajah Reddick

Processioned the Line between Daniel Pugh and Elizabeth Allen both Parties present, likewise Thomas Wiggons and Stephen Parker

Processioned the Line between Daniel Pugh and William Waters both Parties present, likewise Thomas Wiggons and Stephen Parker

Processioned the Line between Daniel Pugh and William Waters both Parties to these Presents, likewise Thomas Wiggons and Andrew Matthews

Processioned the Line between Daniel Pugh and Thomas Wiggons both Parties present likewise William Waters and Andrew Matthews.

Processioned the Line between Daniel Pugh and William Hughs, William Hughs refuses or neglecting present Moses Benton George Williams and Jessie Williams.

Processioned the Line between John Benton and Moses Parker, John Benton Present.

Processioned the Line between John Benton and Caleb Pelson present James Parker and Elijah Benton. (2)

Processioned the Line between the King and James Parker present Elijah Benton and Caleb Polson.

Processioned the Line between John Williamson and James Parker both present, Elijah Benton Caleb Polson.

Processioned the Line between King and John Williamson, John Williamson Present, James Parker present.

Processioned the Line between James Parker and Elijah Benton both parties present.

Processioned the Line between Dorthy Smith and William Truewathan Both present likewise Amos Smith.

Processioned the Line between Dorthy Smith and Samuel Powell Both present likewise Peter Parker.

Processioned the Line Between Darthy Smith and Henry Morgan both present likewise Peter Parker

Processioned the Line between Henry Morgan and Samuel Powell both Parties present, likewise Peter Parker.

Processioned the Line between Samuel Powell and William Truewathan both present, likewise Peter Parker.

Processioned the Line for William Truewathan present Peter Parker and Henry Morgan.

Processioned a Line between Ephroditus Boys & William Waters present both Parties likewise Daniel Parker John Harris

Processioned the Line between John Kittrel and William Huggs John Kittrel Present, William Huggs neglecting or Refusing present George Kittrel Jesse Williams.

Processioned the line between John Kittrel & Jane Williams both Parties present likewise George Kittrel

Processioned the Line between William Huggs & ~~Jane Williams & both Parties~~ Present

Processioned the Line between William Huggs and Mary Vann both Present

(3)

Processioned the Lines of William Hughes all Entered Met
after they were forwarned by John Bitterell
Processioned the Lines of John Vaun he himself present
Processioned all the Lines Mary Vaun she present
Processioned the Line between Mary Seward & George Williams
both present Likewise Joseph Figg
Processioned the Lines between George Williams and the
King George Williams and Joseph Figg
Processioned the line between Mary Seward & the King
George Williams present
Processioned the line between Mary Seward & Laurance
Baker both present Likewise George Williams
Processioned the Line between Laurance Baker and the
King Laurance Baker present Likewise William Daniel
Processioned the Lines of John Lewis Edward Vaun present
Processioned the Line Between Abraham Lacitor Andrew
Lord present the parties John Brinkley & Elizah Benton
Processioned the Lines Between Elizah Benton and
Abraham Lacitor present both Parties Elizah Bird
& John Wolb likewise
Processioned the Line Between Elizah Benton & Lemuel
Powell present Elizah Benton.

William Powell } Returns
Richard Felton }

According to the Order of Vestry We have processioned all the Land that is within our Bounds, Processioned by us

Jacob Odom

Joames Bradey

(4)

Feb^ry 7th 1756 Edward Warren his Land dun; Demcey Buckes his Land dun present Edward Vann and Joseph Waren

Edward Vann his Land dun James Bradey his Land dun present Jacob Bucks Edward Vann & James Bradey

Feb 9th 1756 Jacob Bucks his Land dun present Demsey Bucks and ~~Jacob~~ Bucks James Bradey and Jacob Odom.

Feb^ry 10th 1756 James Ellis Senior his Land dun James Ellis Junr his Land dun James Baker his Land dun; Samuel Baker his Land dun, present James Ellis James Baker Richard Baker and John Odom.

Feb^ry 10th 1756 William Jones Land dun, John Odom his Land dun.

Jeathro Harrel his Land dun, present John Odom and William Robard Knight James Ellis Jethro Harrel

Feby 11th John Parker his Land dun, John Parker his other Land dun present John Parker John Odom James Ellis.

Roberd Rogers his Land dun

Feb^ry 14 1756 Henry Goodmans his Land dun Joel Goodman his Land dun James Brady his Land dun Edward Warren his Land dun Isaac Pipken his Land dun, William Goodman present Henry Robert Rogers Joel Goodman Edward Warren Isaac Pipken William Goodman

Feb^ry 14th 1756 William Smith his Land dun, Francis Brinkley his Land dun, present Frances Brinkley, Robert Jones William Smith James Jones; William Felton ~~his~~ Land dun.

Robert Knight his Land dun, James Ellis Junr his Land dun, Thomas Langstone Land dun, Francis Langstone Land dun, present Robert Knight William Felton, Thomas Langston.

Feb^ry 27th 1756 John Odom his Land dun present Edward Warren

(5)

7

Febry 27 1756 Edward Hare his Land dun; John Lewis his Land dun, Joseph Bradley his Land dun; John Duckins his Land dun, Elizabeth Hartlock hur Land dun, present Edward Hare, John Lewis, Joseph Bradey, John Duckins, Elizabeth Hartlock

Febry 28th 1756 Robert Rogers his Land dun, Stephen Rogers his Land dun; Thomas Langstone his Land dun, present Robert Rogers, Stephen Rogers, Thomas Langstone

Febry 28 1756 John Parker his Land dun; William Vinfleet his Land dun present John Parker William Vinfleet

Febry 28 1756 Thomas Harreles his Land dun James Bradays his Land dun & William Goodmans Lands dun, Alexander Carter his Land dun present Stephen Rogers Elexander Carter.

March the 2 1756 Thomas Odom his Land dun; Thomas Hareles his Land dun, Ephraditus Gones his Land dun, Jethro Harrel his Land dun, James Ellis his Land dun, John Odoms Swamp dun, Present Ephraditus Gones, Jethro Harrel John Odom, John Odom Joseph Tomes

March 11th 1756 Willis Reddick his Land dun, Stephen Shepard too tracts dun, Jacob Odam his Land dun, Edward Vann his Land dun, present Willis Reddick, Stephen Shepard Joseph Noflet, Daniel Lasiter

March the 16 1756. James Tomes his Land dun ffrancis Brinkley ~~his Land~~ dun; Present Robert Tomes and James Tomes and Francis Brinkley

Thomas Piland his Land dun, Edward Piland his Land dun Joseph Noflet present Thomas Piland Edward Piland James Piland Joseph Noflet

(6)

(8)

March 26 1756 R Jacob Mann his Land dun, present George Man, Jacob Rogers Jacob Mann Elizabeth Mann.

March 29 1756 R Henry Backer his Land dun, at his Mill Joyning to Noflet present Joseph Noflet Henery Baker, James Bray Baker,

Febry the 21th 1756 Edward Hare Junr. his Land dun, Philip Pepkins his Land dun Moses Odom his Land dun, present Edward Hare Isaac Pepkins Moses Odom

Febry the 25. 1756 Edward Hare his Land dun, Edward Hare his Land dun, Isaac Williams his Land dun, present Edward Hare, Isaac Williams. Steward Pipkins his Land dun, Robend Parker his Land dun present Steward Pipkin, Stephen Shepard and Robert Parker,

March 29 1756 R Edward Hare his other Land dun James Connor his Land dun present Edward Hare, James Connor

March 27 1756 R Jacob Odom his Land dun, Joseph Knowflet, his Land dun, James Curee his Land dun, present Joseph Knowflet, Thomas Langstone, Thomas Piland his Land, William Frier his Land dun,

March 26 1756 R Robert Knight and William Jones their Land dun, present George Vann

Jacob Odom, Robert Knight, John Porter his Land dun

North Carolina }
Chowan County } Persuant to an Order of Vestry bearing date the 25th Day of October last, for the Processioning of Lands We have agreeable thereto Processioned James Hintons, William Hayses, David Fulks, John Waltons, Gabriel Lacetors, Jethorn Lacetors, Maxemelion Minshews, Richard Minshews, Aaron Blanshards, Micajah Blanshards, Timothy Waltons, William Walton Sen, William Walton Jun.r James Costens, Thomas Hotts, Richard Bonds, John Lacetors, James Browns, Joseph Measels and Aaron Measels' Lands

Robert Lacetor
Moses Lacetor

In Complyance to an Order of Vestry dated the 25th of Octobe 1755 We the Subscribers have processioned all the Bounds of Land according to order peaceable except a line between Benjamine Blanchard and John Watson Stopt by the said Blanchard

francis Saunders
John Miners

January the 10th 1756
Processioned pursuant to order, by Abner Eason and Guy Hill Junr
Between Thomas Walton and Nathaniel Spivey
Between Nathaniel Spivey and Jacob Spivey
Between Jacob Spivey and Aron Hill Jun.r
Between Jacob Spivey and Aron Hill Sen.r
Between Timothy Walton and Aron Hill Sen.r
Between Macaiath Blanchard & Aron Hill Sen.r
Between Aron Hill Sen.r and Aron Hill Jun.r

Between Jacob Spivey and Ephraim Blanchard
Between Ephraim Blanchard and Benjamin Blanchard
Between Macajah Blanchard and Benjamin Blanchard
Between Amous Blanchard and Aron Blanchard
Between James Griffin and Joseph Griffin
Between James Griffen and Abraham Hill
Between James Griffen and Guy Hill
Between Guy Hill and Jonas Spivey
Between Jonas Spivey and James Griffen
Between Jonas Spivey and Joal Spivey
Between Joal Spivey and Moses Rountree
Between Joal Spivey and Abraham Hill
Between Joal Spivey and Edward Berryman
Between George Eason and Benjamin Berryman
Between Samuel Stallings and James Scot
Between George Eason and James Scot
Between James Scot and Benjamin Berryman
Between George Eason and Benjamin Berryman
Between George Eason and Abner Eason
Between Abner Eason and Edward Berryman
Between Abner Eason and Guy Hill
Between Guy Hill and Abraham Hill
Between Abraham Hill and Edward Berryman
Between Guy Hill and Moses Roundtree
Between John Evans and Joseph Griffen
Between Joseph Griffen and William Walton
Between William Walton and Edward Trotman
Between Edward Trotman and Moses Rountree
Between Jacob Doctor and Moses Pearce
Between Luke Sumner and Joal Hunter
Between Elisha Hunter and William Hunter

41

(9)

Between Elisha Hunter and Samuel Green
Between Samuel Green and William Eason
Between William Eason and Joseph Hurdlee
Between Joseph Hurdlee and Jacob Doctor
Between Jacob Spieght and George Eason Senr

Persuant to an Order of Vestry dated the 15th of October 1755 We the Subscribers have processioned all the Lands within the District mentioned in the said Order as by a=bove List dated the 6th of April 1756 pr Abner Eason
Jury Hill

North Carolina Chowan County April the 5th 1756
Persuant to an Order of Vestry past the 25th of October 1755 We the Subscribers being appointed processioners to procession a Canton laid out for them by the said Vestry Beginning at Bennitts Creek Bridge so along Bennitts Creek Road to Catharine Creek Bridge so down the said Creek to the River thence up the River to Bennitts Creek thence up the said Creek to the afd Bridge And Accordingly We met and Qualifyed And then Processioned all the Lands within the said Canton; Only Mr James Wilson and Henry Hill refuses to Procession with Jesse Hunter and Edward Boyland refuses to procession with James Wilson

Benjamin Blanshard
Jesse Hunter

12 In Persuance to an Order of Vestry bearing Date the 15 of December 1755 We processioned all the Lands in our Bounds as follows. (10)

Processioned the Line between James Wilson and George Peland Both Parties present

Processioned the Line between George Peland and John Alston both Parties present

Processioned the Line between George Peland and Henry Baker both Parties Present

Processioned the Line between Henry Baker and John Alston both parties present

Processioned the Line between Henry Baker and William Hays both Parties present

Processioned the Lines between Henry Baker and William Hays both Parties present

Processioned the Lines between John Alston and James Brown Sen both Parties present

Processioned the Line between John Alston and William Hays Sen both parties present

Processioned the Line between John Alston and Bathsheba Sumner both parties present

Processioned the Line between Thomas Sumner and John Alston both parties present

Processioned the Line between William Daniel and William Riddick both parties present

Processioned the Line between William Riddick and John Maddery both parties present

Processioned the Line between William Riddick and Lamuel Baker both parties Present

137

(11)

Processioned the Line between Henry Baker and John Madanee both parties present

Processioned the Line between Laurence Baker and Mary Soward both Parties Present

Processioned the Line between George Piland and James Piland both Parties Present Wm Daniel
James Piland

Pursuant to an order of Vestry dated October 15th 1756 We the Subscribers have processioned all the Lands Marks within the district in the said Order mentioned as follows Viz

Between Whome	Persons Present
William Powell and George Gordon	the same
Marmaduke Norflet & George Gordon	the same
Ditto and Isaac Hill	the Same
Lemuel Powel and Ditto	Isaac Hill
Elizabeth Norflet & Lemuel Powell	David Jones
Ditto and David Jones	Ditto
Ditto and Moses Hair	Ditto
Thomas Parker & Ditto	Ditto
Peter Brinkley and David Jones	Ditto
George Gordon & Ditto	Ditto and Peter Brinkley
Ditto and Francis Powell	Ditto
James Jones and Ditto	Ditto Jethro Peale
Demsey Jones and Thomas Wiggens	Jethro Benton and Jesse Peale
Jesse Peale and Daniel Pugh	Ditto
Ditto and Jethro Benton	Ditto
Jethro Benton and Marmaduke Norflet	Ditto and Daniel Benton
Daniel Pugh and Ditto	Ditto & Ditto
Epaphroditus Benton & Jethro Benton	Ditto and Ditto
James Parker and Ditto	Ditto and Ditto
Joseph Jones and William Parker	Thomas Parker

(12)

(3) William Parker and Wm. Naylet — Thomas Parker
Thomas Parker and Wm. Parker — Joseph Jones
Joseph Jones & Edward Arnell William Parker
Dempsey Sumner & Benja. Parker Jethro Benton
Ditto and James Parker. — Ditto
Thomas Higgens and Thomas Frazer Benjamin Parker
Benjamin Parker & Ditto: Thomas Higgens
Thomas Higgens & John Knight Hugos Edwengame
John Knight & Edw. Arnell . Thomas Wiggens
Luke Sumner & Saml. Sumner — William Sumner
William Sumner & Ditto .. Hugos Edwengame
Edward Arnell & Thomas Wiggens — John Knight

April 2d. 1756
William Powell
Edward Arnell

February 4th 1756
Then Processioned all the Lands of William Freeman Joseph Taylor Richard Freeman Ralph Outlaw Jonathan Walliss Hanse Hoffler James Symner.

5th Processioned the Lands of Charles Roundtree Thomas Walton Christen Ward Thomas Roundtree Amos Hobbs William Willis John Hobbs Guy Hobbs.

6th Processioned the Lands of Thomas Hobbs Mary Jason Lewis Outlaw.

7th Samuel Perry's Land David Sumner George White Stephen Thomas Joseph Doblin.

15/

15th March processioned the Lands of Richard Gant, Rubin Hinton, Richard Chapell, Christen Ward, Edward Nugent, Brizil Ward,

17th Thomas Ward, Lewis Ward, Thomas Ward Jr, Joseph Ward, Christine Ward, Ann Ward. (13)

18th Benjamin Ward, Alexander Maclony, James Ward, John Ward, Samuel Parks, Joseph Coplen, Edward Nugent, John Gooding, Richard Gooding, Joseph Gooding, James Sumner, Daniel Rogers, Joseph Windlo, John Hodson.

20th Timothy Lilley, Joseph Lilley, Lary Holaway, Hardy Hurdle, Richard Pelton, James Eason, Mary Eason, Dinar Coplen, Richard Hurdle, James Scott, Thomas Garrett, Thomas Hobbs, Barnaby Hobbs

Pursuant to and in Obedience of an Order of the Vestry of St Pauls Parish appointing us the Subscribers Processioners to Procession all the Lands Included between Catherines Creek the Sandy Run and Perquimans Road and to make a return thereof to the County Court &c This may certify that We have accordingly processioned the Same according to the within List of the Owners Names Witness our Hands This Sixth day of April 1756

James Sumner

Richard Freeman

An Account of the Lines Processioned by Luke White and Wm Boyd and fresh Marked Vizt Between Richard Garrett, John Bacor and William Boyd from Indian Creek to Rockahock Swamp then from a Gum standing in the Edge of the said Swamp to a Gum in the Horse Pen Pecosin Between Samuel Woodward and William Boyd down a Line of Markt Trees between John Walter and Boyd

16 Present Samuel Woodward John Wallis then Between John Wallis and Samuel Woodward to Woodwards Corner Tree an Old Poplar now Markt, a Small Oake, Woodward and Wallis present. A part of Wallis's disputed by Edward Woodward from the aforesaid Corner Tree to the Horse pen Poquosin, then from from the Poly Bridge Swamp along lines Between William Boyds and the Woodwards Lands and Between the Said Lands and Some Land held by William Lewis then Between the Woodward and Miles Halsey from the Didy House Down to the Rich Neck Swamp p Edward Woodward and Miles Halsey present then from Rockahock Creek along a line of Marked Trees between Samuel McGuire and Miles Halsey they present then between Samuel McGuire and Abraham Norfleet along a Line of Marked Trees down to Rockahock Trees McGuire and Norfleet present Then Between Jacob Pruit and William Boyd they present along a line of Marked Trees then round between the Lands held by William Lewis and Jacob Pruitt Francis James Orphans and Shadrick Bunch a line of Marked Trees to the Land Entred by Jesse Bunch Present — Shadrick Bunch and Pruitt then Between the Entred Land and Shadrick Bunch a line of Marked Trees Down to the river present then from the River present Between Bunches Entry and Thomas Hubbards a line of Marked Trees to Harveys Corner Tree then along a line Hubbard David Ambrose present of Marked Trees Round Hubbards and Pridhams Land to McCravens Corner Tree then along a line of Marked Trees to a loose Tree on the River Near the house landing then from Rockahock Creek along a line of Marked Trees between James Luin and McCravens Land to Luins Corner Tree present Lewis Jones then Between Lewis Jones and Luins to the Miry Branch Lewis Jones —

(14)

present then between Lewis Jones and David Ambrose
from Rockahock Creek to their Corner Tree then round
the Rest of ambroses Lines to Rockahock Creek then (15)
from the river between Lukes White and William
Boyd a line of Marked Trees to the Poly Bridge
Swamp then between Lukes White and John
Wallis a line of marked Trees to the Rocky Branch
then Between Luke White and John Campbell Esqr along
a line of Marked Trees to the River and no further

pr Wm Boyd
Luke White

In Persuance to an Order of Vestry Barring Date the 15th of December
1756 We have processioned all the following lands in our Bounds as
follows Processioned ye Lines between Elisha Hunter and John Gordon
Processioned ye Lines between Jacob Hunter and Samuel Harrel parties pres
Processioned ye Lines between Aaron Lassiter and William Rice
Processioned the Lines between John Rice and Judah Jones
Processioned the Lines between Samuel Harrel and Wm Boyd
Processioned the Lines between Aaron Lassiter and Thomas Fullington
Processioned the Lines between Josiah Granberry and John Harris
Processioned the Lines between Robert Powell and Abraham Hill
Processioned the Lines between John Davis and the Widow Boyce
Processioned the Lines between Abraham Hill and the Widow Hinton
Processioned the Lines between William Rice and Judah Jones
Processioned the Lines between Reuben Philips and Moses Speight
Processioned the Lines between Daniel Pugh and James Wiggins
Processioned the Lines between James Philips and Josiah Small
Processioned the Lines between Daniel Pugh and Richard Bond
all Parties Present pr us

John Rice
Samuel Harrell

18/ Janary the 29th 1756
Processioned for William Goodman beginning at
a Pine a fore and aft tree in a Running Line to a pine a Corner tree between (16)
William Goodman and William Lang a Running Line to a pine a Corner
Tree a Running to a Gum a Corner tree a Running Line to a Pine a Corne
tree of James Lang present Robert Rogers and John Webb a runing Line
between William Goodman and Robert Rogers to a Pine Corner Tree of Wm
Goodman a running Line tree to the Road present Isaac Pipkin and Robert
Rogers, Processioned for Isaac Pipkin a running Line to the Run of the Bever
Dam to a Pine a Corner tree of Isaac Pipkins a running Line between Wm
Goodman and Isaac Pipkin to the Road present William Gattling Jas
and Jno Webb beginning at the Senter three Pines of Thomas Barns a
Running Line tree to the senter of three Pines of John Winborns Line a Run-
ing Line to a Red Oak a Corner tree of Frances Brinkley Line to a White Oak a
Corner Tree of John Odom Line a running Line to a pine tree a Corner tree of
John Odoms Present John Skiner and Jacob Odom a running Line from a
Red Oak to a Pine a Corner tree of Thomas Barns a running Line between John
Odom and Thomas Barnes to the Senter of three Trees Present Jno Skinner and
Jacob Odom beginning at a White Oak a Corner tree of James Thomas a Running
Line to a White Oak a corner tree then a running Line to a White Oak to a Corner tree
then a Running Line to a White Oak a Corner tree of John Skinner then a runing
Line to a Branch, Present Jas Odom Jno Odom and William Felton Junr beginning
at a Water Oak a Corner tree of Francis Brinkley a Running Line to a Gum
Tree of Jas Thomas then a running Line to a Pine a Corner Tree o Robert
Thomas a Running Line between Jno Elles and Francis Brinkley to a Pine
a Corner tree of Jno Elles then a running Line to a pine a Corner tree then a running
Line to a Maple a Corner tree of John Elles present James Thomas and Frances
Brinkley beginning at a Hickrey a Corner tree of Robert Nights then a
Running Line to Edward Hare Line present William Jones. Beginning at
a White Oak a Corner Tree of Mary Barnes a running Line to Edward
Warrens Line present Thomas Barns beginning at a gum a Corner tree
between William Gattling & Edward Hare a running Line to a Hickrey a
Corner tree of Moses Hare then a running Line between William Gattings
and Moses Hare to a Gum a Corner tree Moses Odoms then a Running Line

Between William Gattling and Moses Odom to a corner Tree of Moses Odom Jur. then a running Line between Moses Odom Jur. and William Gattings to a corner tree at white of Isaac Williams then a Running Line between Moses Odam Junior and Isaac Williams to the road Present Edward Gatling & William Gatling Junior — beginning at a pine a Corner Tree Willis Reddick then a running line to a Water Oak a Corner tree of William Long then a running line Between James Long & Willis Reddick to the Virginia Line then a running line between Willis Reddick & Daniel Marsh present William Rogers & James Long all these Lines peaceably Processioned

Edward Ware Junior
Joseph Speight

(17)

Aprill 2d Day 1756

In Obedience to an order of Vestry we the Subscribers have Processioned all the Lands Marks we knows of or had been showed in the District as Laid at as followeth Between Adam Vits and Jacob Odam in presents Odam Vits and Jacob Odum and John Green & Between James Euro and Jacob Odam in presents James Euro and John Green Between Richard Parker and Mary Green in presents John Green Senr. and John Green Junior Between John Sparkmon and Richard Parker in presents John Sparkmon and John Green and James Euro Between James Euro And Mary Green In Presents James Euro and John Green and John Sparkman In presents John Green and James Euro Between James Euro and John Sparkmon in presents John Green & James Euro Between Mary Green and William Smith in Presents John Green and William Smith Between the Green and John Sparkmon

(18)

(K) April 5, 1756

Pursuant to an Order of the Vestry of St. Pauls Parish we the Subscribers Have Processioned all the land mark within the Destrict in the Order mentioned as appeared by the Annext. Dated April 5th 1756

William Cowell
Richard Felton

(19)

Procesoned the Line between peter parker &
William truewathan both partys present Likewise
Henory morgan
Made and Procesoned aline for peter parker kings
Land Joyning henery morgan william truewathan
Present
Procesoned the Line between the king & william
Truewathan: truewathan present Likewise
Peter parker
Procesoned the line between Peter parker &
Daniel parker both parties present Likewise
Elijah benton
Procesoned the Line between Daniel parker &
The king Daniel parker present Likewise
William Elijah benton

Procesoned the Line [illegible] Ephraim [illegible]
Richard baker both both present Likewise william
truewathan
Prosesoned the Line between John kittrel & Richard
Baker both parties present Likewise William truew[illegible]
Procesoned ye Line between Richard felton and Daniel
Parker both present Likewise John hains
Procesoned the line between Daniel parker Richard baker
both partys present Likewise william woters
[illegible] Richard Baker & peter parker
Procesoned [illegible]
both present Likewise [illegible] hains william waters
Procesoned the Line between Richard baker & John hains both
Partys present likewise william waters Daniel parker
Procesoned the Line between John kittrel & John hains both partys
Present Likewise Richard baker and John kittrel
Procesoned the Line between John hains & the king hains present
Likewise william worters Richard baker

(20)

Prosessioned the Line between George Williams and Moses Benton present both Parties Present allso Daniel Pugh and John Benton Son of Moses

Prossessioned the Line between Daniel Pugh and George Williams both Parties Present Likewise Wm Daniel John Hambelton and John Benton Junr

Prossessioned Daniel Pugh ... Likewise Wm Daniel John ... Son of George Williams

Prosessioned the Line between Daniel Pugh and William Powell Present both Parties Present likewise William Daniel & Henry Smith

Prosessioned the Line between Wm Daniel & Henry Smith both Parties Present Likewise Daniel Pugh Wm Daniel Jonathan Baker

Prossessioned the Line between Henry Smith and Daniel Pugh both Parties Present Likewise Wm Daniel & Jonathan Baker

Prosessioned the line between Micajah Reddick and Thos Harrel both Parties Present Thos Wiggins & Richard Brothers and Daniel Pugh

Prosessioned the Line between Micajah Reddick and Wm Jonathan Present both Parties ... Pugh Thos Wiggins and Richd Brothers

Prosessioned the Line between Micajah Reddick and Dorathy Smith Present both Parties Likewise Danl Pugh Thos Wiggins and Richard Brothers

Prossessioned the Line between Thos Harrel & Richard Felton both Parties Present Likewise Wm Daniel

(21)

Professioned the Line between William Waters and Richard Brothers both Parties Present likewise Danl. Pugh and Wm. Daniel

Professioned the Line between Richard Felton & Richard Baker both Parties Present likewise Danl. Pugh & John Kitterall

Professioned the Line between John Kitterall and Richard Baker both Parties Present likewise Danl. Pugh & Stephen Parker

Professioned the Line between John Kitterall & Wm. Waters both Parties Present likewise Danl. Pugh and Richard Baker

Professioned the Line between Richard Baker & John Kitterall both Parties Present likewise Danl. Pugh [illegible] Stephen Parker

Professioned the Line between [illegible] Waters and Richd. Baker both Parties [illegible] likewise Danl. Pugh [illegible]

Professioned the Line between [illegible] Waters and Richd. Parker both Parties Present likewise Danl. Pugh [illegible]

Professioned the Line between Richard Baker and Richd. Parker both Parties Present likewise Danl. Pugh & Thos. Wiggins

Professioned the Line between Epaphroditus Boyce and Richd. Baker both Parties Present likewise Danl. Pugh & Thos. Wiggins

Professioned the Line between Richd. Parker & Epaphroditus Boyce both Parties Present likewise Danl. Pugh & Thos. Wiggins

Professioned the Line between Daniel Pugh & Epaphroditus Boyce both Parties Present likewise Richd. Baker & Thos. Wiggins

Professioned the Line between Daniel Pugh & Richd. Brothers both Parties Present likewise Thos. Wiggins [illegible]

Professioned the Line between Daniel Pugh & Elizabeth Allen both Parties Present likewise Thos. Wiggins and Stephen Parker

Professioned the Line between Daniel Pugh & Wm. Waters both Parties Present likewise Thos. Wiggins & Andrew Matthews

(22)

Processioned the line between Daniel Pugh and Thos Wiggins both parties present likewise Wm Watters & Andrew Matthews

Processioned the line between Daniel Pugh and Wm Hughs Daniel Pugh present Wm Hughs Refusing or Neglecting Present Moses Benton George Williams & Jessie Williams

Processioned the line between John Benton & Moses Parker John Benton present

Processioned the Line between John Benton & Caleb Polson present James Parker Elijah Benton

Processioned the Line between the king & James Parker present Elijah Benton Caleb Polson

Processioned the Line between John Williamson & James Parker both present Elijah Benton Caleb Polson

Processioned the Line between the king & John Williamson John Williamson present James Parker present

Processioned the Line between James Parker & Elijah Benton both partys present

Processioned the Line between Dorthy Smith & William Treewatham both present likewise James Smith

Processioned the Line between Dorithy Smith & Ismail Powel both present Likewise Peter Parker

Processioned the Line between Dorthy Smith & Henery Morgan both partys present Likewise Peter Parker

Processioned the Line between Henery Morgan & Ismail Powell both partys present Likewise Peter Parker

Processioned the Line between Ismaill Powell William Treewatham both present Likewise Peter Parker

Processioned a line for William Treewatham present Peter Parker Henery Morgan

Porcessioned the line between Epehroditus boys & William waters present both parties likewise Daniel Parker John hains (23)

Porcessioned the line between John kittrel & william huggs John kittrel present william huggs neglecting or Refusing present George kittrel Isser williams

Porcessioned the line between John kittrel Jane williams both parties present Likewise George kittrel

Porcessioned the line between william huggs & Jan williams both parties present

Porcessioned the line between william huggs & mary vann Both present

Porcessioned the lines of william hughs all but one marked after they ware forwarn by John kittrel

Porcessioned the Lines John Varner him present

Porcessioned all the Lines mary vann She present

Porcessioned the Line between mary Soward & George williams both present Likewise Joseph figg

Porcessioned the Line between george williams & the king George williams present Likewise Joseph figg

Porcessioned the Line between mary Soward & the King George williams Present

Porcessioned the Line between mary Soward & Larane Baker both present Likewise ~~william~~ George williams

Porcessioned the Line Larane baker & and the King Larane Barker present Likewise William Daniel

Porcessioned the Line of John Luis Edward vann present

Processioned the Line Between Abraham Lacitor & my Self present ~~both~~ parties John Brinkley & Elijah Benton

Processioned the Line Between Elijah Benton & Abraham Lucitor present Both Parties, Elijah Bird & John Webb Likewise

Processioned the Line Between Elijah Benton & Samuel Powel present Elijah Benton

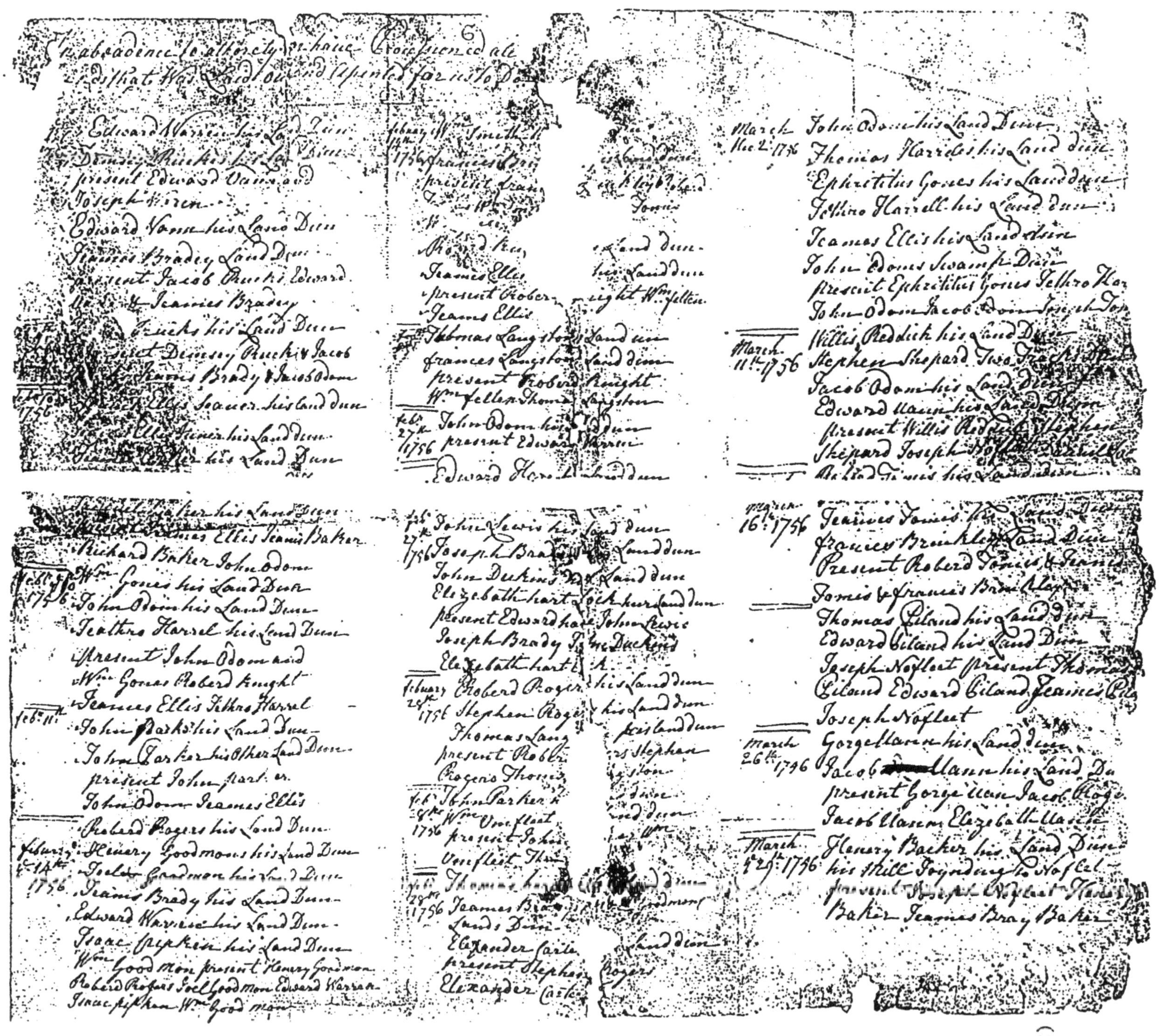

In abedience to athority we have Procesioned all
that Was Land ou[illegible] and apointed for us to do

Edward Warren his Land Dun
Demsey Rucks his Land Dun
present Edward Vann and
Joseph Vann
Edward Vann his Land Dun
Jeames Bradey Land Dun
present Jacob Rucks Edward
[illegible] & Jeames Brady
[illegible] Rucks his Land Dun
present Demsey Rucks & Jacob
[illegible] Jeams Brady & Jacob Odom
1756 [illegible] Ellis Jeames his Land dun
[illegible] Ellis Jenir his Land dun
[illegible] his Land Dun

febuary 14th 1756 Wm Smith [illegible]
frances [illegible]
present fran[illegible]
[illegible] Land dun
[illegible] Land Dun
Jeames Ellis [illegible] his Land dun
present Rober[illegible] [illegible] Wm fellen
Jeames Ellis
Thomas Langston [illegible] Land dun
frances Langston [illegible] Land dun
present Robert Knight
Wm fellen Thomas Langston
feb 27th 1756 John Odom his [illegible] Land dun
present Edward [illegible]
Edward [illegible] Land dun

March the 2 1756 John Odom his Land Dun
Thomas Harrell his Land dun
Ephriditus Jones his Land dun
Jethro Harrell his Land dun
Jeames Ellis his Land dun
John Odoms Swamp Dun
present Ephriditus Jones Jethro Har[illegible]
John Odom Jacob Odom [illegible]
March 11th 1756 Willis Reddick his Land Dun
Stephen Shepard Two Tracts [illegible]
Jacob Odom his Land Dun
Edward Mann his Land Dun
present Willis Reddick Stephen
Shepard Joseph [illegible]
[illegible] his Land dun

[illegible] his Land Dun
present Jeames Ellis Jeams Baker
Richard Baker John Odom
feb 8th 1756 Wm Jones his Land Dun
John Odom his Land Dun
Jeathro Harrel his Land Dun
present John Odom and
Wm Jones Robert Knight
Jeames Ellis Jethro Harrel
feb 11th John Parker his Land Dun
John Parker his other Land Dun
present John Park[illegible]
John Odom Jeames Ellis
Robert Rogers his Land Dun
febuary 14th 1756 Henery Goodmon his Land Dun
Joel Goodmon his Land Dun
Jeams Brady his Land Dun
Edward Warren his Land Dun
Isaac Pipkin his Land Dun
Wm Goodmon present Henery Goodmon
Robert Rogers Joel Goodmon Edward Warren
Isaac Pipkin Wm Goodmon

feb 27th 1756 John Lewis his Land dun
Joseph Brady his Land dun
John Duckins his Land dun
Elezebath hart [illegible] her Land dun
present Edward hart John Lewis
Joseph Brady [illegible] Duckins
Elezebath hart [illegible]
febuary 28th 1756 Robert Rogers his Land dun
Stephen Rogers his Land dun
Thomas Lang[illegible] his Land dun
present Robert [illegible] Stephen
Rogers Thomas [illegible]
feb 28th 1756 John Parker [illegible]
Wm Vinfleet [illegible] Land dun
present John [illegible] Wm
Vinfleet Thomas [illegible]
feb 28th 1756 Thomas [illegible] Land dun
Jeames Bra[illegible] Goodmon
Land Dun
Elexander Carter Land dun
present Stephen Rogers
Elexander Carter

March 16th 1756 Jeames Jones his Land Dun
frances Brinkley Land Dun
Present Robert Jones & Jeames
Jones & frances Brinkley
Thomas Piland his Land dun
Edward Piland his Land Dun
Joseph Nofleet present Thomas
Piland Edward Piland Jeames Pi[illegible]
Joseph Nofleet
March 26th 1756 Gorge Mann his Land dun
Jacob Mann his Land Dun
present Gorge Mann Jacob Mann
Jacob Mann Elezebath Mann
March 29th 1756 Henery Backer his Land Dun
his Mill Joyning to Nofleet
present Joseph Nofleet Henery
Baker Jeames Bray Baker

(2

(25)

1756 Edward Hare his Land Due
Philip Pipkins his Land Due
Moses Odom Land Due
present Edward Hare Isaac Pipkin
Moses Odom
Moses Hare his Land due
Isaac Williams his Land Due
present Moses Hare Isaac Williams
February 25 1756 Edward Hare his Land Due
Edward Hare his Land Due
Isaac Williams his Land due
present Edward Hare
Isaac Williams
Stephen Shepard his Land due
Robert Parker his Land due
present Edward Pipkin
Stephen Shepard and
Robert Parker
Edward Hare his other Land due
1756 James Conner his Land due
present Edward Hare James Conner
Jacob Odom his Land due
Joseph Knowsfleet his Land due
James Curse his Land due
present Joseph Knowsfleet
Thomas Langstones Thomas Riland
his Land due Wm Frier his Land due
Robert Knight & Wm Jones there
Land due present George [illegible]
Jacob Odom Robert Knight
John Porter his Land [illegible]

According to the Order [illegible]
processioned all the Land[illegible]
[illegible] by
Jacob Odom
James Brady

January the 10th: 1756

Processioned Pursuant to order: by Abner Eason & Grey Hill

Lines Between Thomas Walton and Nathinel Spivey (26)

Between Nathinel Spivey and Jacob Spivey

Between Jacob Spivey and Aron Hill Junr.

Between Jacob Spivey and Aron Hill Senr.

Between Timothy Walton and Aron Hill Senr.

Between Micajah Blanchard and Aron Hill Junr.

Between Aron Hill Senr. ~~and~~ Aron Hill Junr.

Between Jacob Spivey and Epharim Blanchard

Between Epharim Blanchard and Benjamin Blanchard

Between Micajah Blanchard and Benjamin Blanchard

Between Amous Blanchard and Aron Blanchard

Between James Griffin and Joseph Griffin

Between James Griffin and Abraham Hill

Between James Griffin and Grey Hill

Between Grey Hill and Jonas Spivey

Between Jonas Spivey and James Griffin

~~Between Jonas Spivey and Joab Spivey~~

Between Joab Spivey and Moses Rountree

Between Joab Spivey and Abraham Hill

Between Joab Spivey and Edward Bereyman

Between George Eason and Benjamin Bereyman

Between Samuel Stallings and James Scot

Between George Eason and James Scot

Between James Scot and Benjamin Bereyman

Between George Eason and Benjamin Bereyman

Between George Eason and Abner Eason

Between Abner Eason and Edward Bereyman

Between Abner Eason and Grey Hill

Between Grey Hill and Abraham Hill

Between Abraham Hill and Edward Bereyman

Between Grey Hill and Moses Rountree

Between John Greens and Joseph Griffin

Between Joseph Griffin and William Walton

Between William Walton and Edward Crolman

Between Edward Crolman and Moses Rountree

(27)

Between Jacob Docton and Moses Pearce
Between Luke Sumner and Joab Hunter
Between Elisha Hunter and William Hunter
Between Elisha Hunter and Samuel Green
Between Samuel Green and William Eason
Between William Eason and Joseph Hurdle
Between Joseph Hurdle and Jacob Docton
Between Isaac Speight and George Eason Senr.

Pursuant to an Order of Vestry Dated the 15th of October 1755 we the Subscribers have processioned all the Lands within the District mentioned in the said Order as by above List Dated the 6th of April 1756 ℘ Abner Eason
Guy Hill

(28)

North Carolina Chowan County April ye 5th 1756

Persuant to an order of Vestry past the 25th of October 1755. Wee the subscribers being appointed processioners to procession a Canton laid out for them by the sd Vestry beginning att Bennets Creek Bridg so along Bennets Creek Road to Cathries Creek Bridg so down the sd Creek to the River thence up the River to Bennets Creek thence up the sd Creek to the afors Bridg. and accordingly we met & qualified and then processioned all the Lands within the sd Canton only Mr James Wilson & Mr Henry Hill Refused to procession with Jesse Huntor. and Edward peyland refuses to procession with Jaames Wilson

Benjaman Blanshard

Jesse Huntor

(29)

January the 29th 1756 Prosessioned for William Goodman begining at apine afore & aft tree In A Runing Line to apine a Corner tree between Wm. Goodman & Wm. Lang a Runing Line to apine a Corner tree a Runing Line to a gum a Corner tree a Runing Line to apine a Corne tree of James Lang present Robert Rogers & John Web A runing Line betwen Wm. Goodman and Robert Rogers to apine a Corner Tree of Wm. Goodman aruning Line to the road present Isaac pipkin & Robert Rogers prosesioned for Isaac Pipkin aruning Lin to the Run of the bever dam to apin a Corner tree of Isaac Pipkins Aruning Line betwene Wm. Goodman & Isaac Pipkin to the Road Present Wm. Gatlling Jor. & Jo.n Webb begining at the Senter of the same Three pines a Runing Line to the Sente of three pines of John Winbourns Line a Runing Line to a Red Oak a Corne tree of Frances Brinkley Line to a White Oak a Corner Tree of John Odom Line a Runing Line to apine a Corne Tree of John Odoms Present John Skiner & Jacob Odom aruning Line from A red Oak to aPine a Corner tree of Thomas Barnes aruning Line Betwene Jo.n Odom & Tho.s Barnes to the Senter of three Trees Present Jo.n Skiner & Jacob Odom begining at a White Oak a Corner Tree of Ja.s Thomas aruning Line to a White oak a Corner Tree then a Runing line to a White Oak a Corner tree of John Skiner then a Runing Line to a branch Present Ja.s Odom Jo.n Odom & Wm. Felton Jor. begining at a Water Oak a Corne tree of Frances Brinkley aruning Line to agum a Corner tree of Ja.s Thomas then a Runing Line to apine a Corner Tree a Robert Thomas A Runing Line betwene Jo.n Ellis & Frances Brinkley to a pine

(30)

a Corner tree of Jo^n. Elles then a Runing Line to a pine a Corne tree then a runing Line to a Maple a Corne tree of John Elles present James Thomas & Francess Brinkley begining at a Hickrey a Corner Tree of Robert Nights then a runing Line to Edward Hare Line present Wm. Jones begining at a Whit Oak a Corner Tree of mary Barnes a Runing Lin to Edward Warrens Line present Thomas Barnes begining at a gum a Corner tree betwen Wm. Gatling & Edward Hare a runing Line to a hickrey a Corner tree of Moses hare then a runing Line betwene Wm. Gatling & Moses Hare to a gum a Corne tree Moses Odoms then a runing Line Betwen Wm. Gatling & moses Odom to a Corne tree of Moses Odoms Jr. then a runing Line betwen Moses Odom Jr. and Wm. Gatling to a Corner tree a White of Isaac Williams then a runing Line betwen Moses Odom Jr. & Isaac William to the Road present Edward Gatling & Wm. Gatling Janr. begining at at a pine a Corner tree Willes Riddick then a runing Line to a Water Oak a Corne tree of Wm. Lang then a runing Line betwen James Lang & Willes Riddick to the Virginia Line then a runing Line betwen Willes Riddick & Dainel March present Wm. Rogers & James Lang all these Lines Peasably Prosesioned

Edward Hare Jur.

Joseph Speight

(31)

April the 2 Day 1756

In Obdance to an order of Vestry we the
Subscribers have processined all the Lands marks we know
of or has bin showed in the Destrict as Laid ~~at~~ att as
followeth Betwene Adam Site and Jacob Odom ~~and~~ in presants
Adam Site and Jacob Odom and Johngreen & Betwene James Eure and
Jacob Odom in presents James Eure and Jacob Odom & William Umflet
Betwene Mary green and Jacob Odom in presents James Eure and Johngreen
Betwene Richard parker and Marygreen in presents Johngreen Sen. and [illegible]
green Sen. Betwene John Sparkmon and Richard parker in presents John Sp[ark]
kmon and and John green and James Eure. Betwene James Eure and Mary gr[een]
In presents James Eure and John green and John Sparkmon Betwene John ~~[illegible]~~
and John Sparkmon in presents Johngreen and James Eure Betwene Johngreen
Eure and John Sparkmon in presents John green and James Eure Betwene James
Mary green and William Smith in presents ~~[illegible]~~ Johngreen and James Eure Betwene ~~[illegible]~~
Betwene Else green and Thomas Sparkmon in presents Thomas Sparkmon
& Johngreen and William Smith Betwene Else green and william felton in
presents Johngreen and Thomas Sparkmon & William Smith Betwene William
felton and Thomas Sparkmon in presents william felton and Thomas Sparkmon
and William Smith Betwene Thomas Harrell and Thomas Sparkmon in
presents Thomas Sparkmon and Thomas Harrell and William felton
Betwene Thomas Harrell and william felton In presents Thomas Harrell
and William felton and William Smith Betwene William Smith and
Soloman green in presents Soloman green and William Smith and Jonathan Ja[mes]
Betwene Soloman green and Thomas Noris in presents Soloman green and
Thomas Noris and William Smith Betwene James Eure and Thomas Noris
in presents Thomas Noris and James Eure Betwene Thomas Noris and
Sam~~[illegible]~~muell Eure in presents Sammuell Eure and Thomas Noris and
James Eure Betwene Samuell Eure and Andrew Hamblenton in presents
Samuell Eure and Andrew Hambleton and Thomas Noris Betwene James
Eure and Andrew Hambleton in presents James Eure and Andrewhambleton
& Thomas Noris Betwene Andrewhambleton and William Umflet
in presents William Umflet and Andrewhambleton and Thomas Harell
Betwene James Eure and William Umflet part Eedon in presents James Eure
and William Umflet and Thomas Harrell Betwene Thomas Harrell in
Epaproditus Jones part don [illegible] in presents Thomas Harell and Epaproditus Jones
and John Odom Betwen Epaproditus Jones and John Odom in presents
John Odom and Epaproditus Jones and Jacob Odom Betwene Jethro Harrell
and Epaproditus Jones part don in presents Jethro Harrell and Epaproditus Jones and John
Odom and Jacob Odom and ~~[illegible]~~ Joseph Jonas

Betweene Thomas Harrell and John green in presents Thomas Harrell and John green and Thomas Sparkman Betweene Thomas Harrell and Mary green in presents Thomas Harrell and John green and Thomas Sparkman Betweene Mary green and Soloman green in presents Soloman green & James Eure Betweene Soloman ~~and~~ green and Jonas Faler in presents Soloman green and Jonas Faler and william Tomas Betweene John green and Jonas Faler in presents Jonas Faler and Soloman green Betweene William Lancton and Jonas Faler ~~and Soloman green~~ in presents William Lancton and Jonas Faler and Soloman green Betweene William Tomas and Jonas Faler in presents Jonas Faler and William Tomas and Soloman green Betweene William Lancton and Mary green in presents william Lancton and Jonas Faler and William Tomas Betweene Ann Skiner and John Butler in presents Lunard Lancton and Jonas Faler and William Lancton Betweene John Butler and Lunard Lancton in presents William Lancton and Lunard Lancton and Jonas Faler Betweene John Butler and John Denver in presents Lunard Lancton and Jonas Faler Betweene John Denve and Thomas Lancton in presents Jonas Faler Betweene Tomas Lancton and Epaproditus Sons in presents Epaproditus Sons and Laranc Lancton and Lunard Lancton Betweene James Elles and ~~[illegible]~~ Epaproditus Sons in presents James Elles and Epaproditus Sons Betweene Edard Sketer and Larance Lanston in presents Larance Lancton and Lunard Lanston and James Eure ~~Joseph Norflet~~ Betweene Josep Norflet and Edard Sketer in presents Jacob Odom and Joseph Norflet and James frier Betweene Joseph Norflet and John Odom in presents Joseph Norflet and Jacob Odom and James frier Betweene John Odom and Jacob Odom in presents Jacob Odom and Joseph Norflet and James frier Betweene ~~[illegible]~~ Edard Arnal and Jacob Odom in presents Jacob Odom and James frier and Joseph Norflet Betweene Jacob Odom and John Simon in presents Jacob Odom and Joseph Norflet and James frier Betweene John folk and Charls Rusil in presents James Eure and Lunard Lanston Betweene Charls Rusil and John Woril in presents James Eure and Lunard Lancton Betweene John Woril and John Clittlin in presents John Citton and John Woril and John Carter and Tomas Sparkmon Betweene John Citton and James Brady in presents Jacob odom and Tomas Sparkmon and John Citton Betweene John Kitterlon and John Carter in presents John Kitterlon and John Carter and Jacob Odom and Stephen Eure Betweene Stephen Eure and John Kitterlon in presents Stephen Eure and John Kitterlon and Joseph Norflet and John Carter Betweene Stephen Eure and Henry Skiner in presents Stephen Eure and Thomas Lancton and John Carter and Thomas Sparkmon Betweene John Carter and ~~John~~ Henry Skiner in presents John Carter and Thomas Sparkmon and Tomas Lanston Betweene James Eure and Tomas Lancton in presents Lunard Lanston and James Eure All Concluded With in my Bounds Excepting Two or Thre Tracks in Precosen be Longin to Sum Persons I know not. all above Duley and Peaseblay Dun With Consent in the Presence of Us

Jeathro Harrell

James ~~[illegible]~~ Eure

At a Vestry Held for St. Pauls Parish at Constants Chappel on Catterd the 25th Day of October 1755. It was Then and There Pursuant To The Law for Settlering The Title and Bounds of Peoples Lands Ordered That Mr. Robert Rodgers and Mr. John Arline be and They are hereby Appointed Processioners and that They do Procession all The Lands Included begining near Moses Parkers on The New Road so along The Said Road to The Road at Sarum Chappel so along Sarum Road to The Cuntry Line & along ye Line to The New Road and That They make Return There of To the County Court in April next According to Law Which They are not to Omit under The Penalty of Five Pounds Each &c — (33)

Luke Sumner Clk V.

Copy.

3

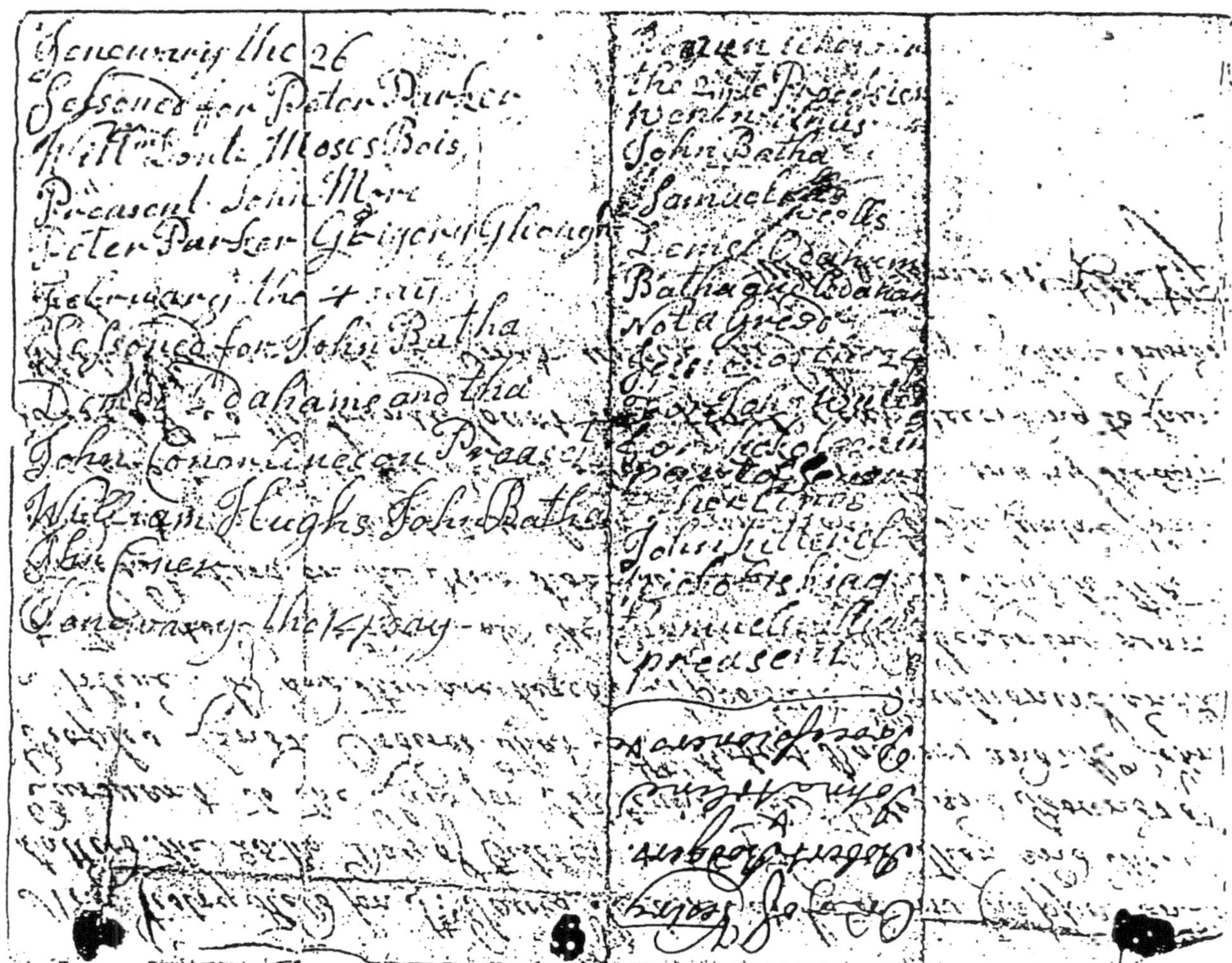
Jenewary the 26
Sessoned for Peter Parker
with Mr Lonte Moses Bois,
Preasent John More
Peter Parker Gregory Gleough
February the 4 day
Sessoned for John Batha
Daniel Odahaine and tha
John Commineacan Preasent
William Hughs John Batha
Jenewary the 4 day

John Batha
Samuel Wells
Daniel Odahaine
Batha
John Fuller
preasent

There present Moses hare and Aaron Odam procession the Line between them Begining at a pine there Corner tree then aLong the Line of marked trees to Moses hare tother Corner pine there present John Drury and Aaron odam and abraham odam processiond the Line Between John Drury and Aaron odam to the Center of three oaks — Then processiond the Line between John Drury and Abraham odam to a Corner white oak near the Road —

Then present Daniel march and abraham odam processiond the Line between them from a Red oak there Line tree aLong the Line to a Corner pine Aarons Odams Corner pine & then a Long the Line between Aaron Odam and Abraham Odam to the Center of three oaks —

Then present Daniel march and Aaron odam processiond the Line from Aaron odams Corner pine along the Line between them two to a Corner pine John weeks Corner processiond to the Short beaver Dam then up the beaverdam to a Line of marked trees to Tom Moriss Corner then a Line of marked trees to the Grate beaverdam present Aaron Odam then present Moses Hare and Edward Hare processiond the Line between them two from a Corner hickory a Long the Line to a Corner pine — present Edward hare and John Lewis processiond the Line between them two from a Corner Gum to a Gum a Corner tree on milses Swamp —

present Thomas Barns and Francis Sanders processiond the Line for Thomas Barns from a Gum his Corner tree then a Long his Line to the Center of three pines then a Long his Line to a white oak his Corner tree —

Present Henry King processiond the Line Between he & Thomas Barns Begining at a pine Kings Corner tree then a Long the Line to a Gum & Kings Corner tree —

present Henry King processiond his Line begining at a Small dead Gum his Corner tree then along his Line to a pine moses hares Corner tree then a Long Kings Line to his one Corner tree a white oak —

present Moses hare and francis Sanders processiond the Line Between Joseph Sprigh and henry King begining at a Red oak a Corner tree then a Long the Line to the head Line then along that to the Long Branch —

(35)

then present moses hare and francis Sanders procession'd the Line for moses hare Begining at a pine on the Side of the flat Cyprus So Down the Sand Banks along a Line of marked trees to the Road — present moses hare & william Speight procession'd begining at a white oak a Corner tree betwen them two then along the Line to a Corner pine then along the Line to Hares Corner tree present william Speight and Francis Sanders procession'd the Line for farncis Sanders begining at a Red oak his Corner then along his Line to a white oak his Corner then a Long his Line to a white oak his Corner tree — present John wollice and Charles King procession'd for John wollice begining at his Corner Gum then a long his Line to his Corner white oak then along his Line to boi yces line then a Long there Line to Charles Kings Corner then present Charles King and Christopher boiyce procession'd the line between them two from King Corner along the Line to Everits Corner pine then along Kings Line of marked trees to his one Corner then present Charles King and francis Sanders & Christopher boiyces procession'd boiyces Line from Everits Corner pine along his Line to his one Corner pine then a Long his Line to hunters Corner then along the Line of marked trees to wollices Line then present John wollice procession'd the Line for him from a white oak his Corner a long his Line of marked trees to a Swamp Caled the Gum Swamp then present william Lang and John weeb James Lang procession'd the Line btween william Lang and James Lang from a Corner pine along the Line of marked trees to the Corner a pine between James Lang and william Goodman to a Corner Red oak Robert Rogerses Corner present James Lang and John Bethey procession'd the Line between them two to a pine on Sarum Road then along the Line betwee Trustum bethey and James Lang to a hickry there Corner and then a Long the Line betweon them two to a pine one the Beatch Swamp there Corner tree.

(36)

present William Speight procession'd for Joseph Speight his Line from a pine ~~James Mayonge~~ William Harriston's Corner along the Line to the miry Branch to a pine

present ~~Edwarren~~ Edward waren and John Lewes procession'd the Line between Joseph Speight and John Lewis from the white oak and Gum to the Center of three pines — then present Thomas Barns and Edward waren processiond the Line between Joseph Speight and Edward warren from the Center of three pines to a Corner pine Speights Corner — then present Thomas Barns Procession'd the Line between Joseph Speight & Thomas Barns from Speights Corner a long the Line to Barnses Corner oak then a long the Line to Barnes Corner a pine in Kings Line — then present Edward hare & John Lewis procession'd the Line between John Lewis and Edward Warren from the Center of three pines along the Line to warrens Corner pine — Then present Ed hare and Ed warren & Thomas Barns procession'd for Ed Hare and Ed warren from a Corner pine a long the Line of marked trees to an oak — Then present Charles King and henry King procession'd the Line Between Joseph Speight & Charles King begining at a pine a Corner of Kings then a long the Line of marked trees to a white oak Speight Corner then a long the Line to a white oak Speight other Corner — then present Francis Sanders & henry King and Ed Hare processiond the Line between Joseph Speight & Francis Sanders begining at a Gum Speights Corner tree then along the Line of marked trees to the Road

present ~~Wi~~ William Vaughn procession'd for him Begining at a magnole his Corner then a long his Line to his outher Corner pine then a long his Line to a popler his Corner then a long his Line ~~to~~ the Gum Swamp —

(37)

All these Lines Peasably Professioned

Edward Hare

Joseph Speight

(38)

(39)

In Obedience to an Order of Vestry Dated October the 23: 1764 We the Possessioners have Processioned all the Land between the flat Branch and the Country line, and along Bennets Creech to the main Road

Lines	Between whom	Who Present	Lines	Between whom	Who Present
	Luke Sumner & Sam: Sumner	the parties present		James Jones & John Gordon	the parties
	Sam Sumner & Elisha Sumner under Age	one party & Luke Sumner		David Jones & Peter Brinkley	the Parties
	Jacob Sumner & Willis Wiggins	one party & Moses Hare		David Jones & Eliz: Norfleet	the Parties
	Edward Arnell & Eliz: Knight	both Parties		Tho: Parker & Moses Hare	the Parties
	Eliz: Knight & Willis Wiggins	one Party & Edward Arnell		Tho: Parker & William Parker	one Party and Moses Hare
	Edward Arnell & Joseph Jones	one Party & Tho: Parker		Epa: Benton & James Parker	the Parties
	Tho: Parker & Edward Arnell	one Party & Joseph Jones		Epa: Benton & Tho: Parker	one Party & Moses Benton
	Edward Arnell & Willis Wiggins	the Parties		Epa: Benton & Jethro Benton	the Parties
	Edward Arnell & James Parker	one Party & John Darden		Jethro Benton & Isaac Benton	one Party & Moses Benton
	John Darden & Willis Wiggins	one Party & Edward Arnell		Isaac Benton & John Reed	one Party & Robt: Rule
	John Darden & James Parker	one Party & Edward Arnell		Joseph Brinkley & Kader Ballard under Age	one Party & Elisha Norfleet
	Edward Arnell & Joseph Jones	one Party & Tho: Parker		Joseph Brinkley & Marmaduke Norfleet	one Party & Elisha Norfleet
	Joseph Jones & William Parker	the Parties		Joseph Brinkley & David Jones	the Parties
	Willis Wiggins & Tho Frazier	the Parties		Joseph Brinkley & Eliz: Norfleet	the Parties
	Demsey Sumner & John Darden	the Parties		David Jones & Marmaduke Norfleet	one Party & Peter Brinkley
	Demsey Sumner & James Parker	the Parties		Marmaduke Norfleet & John Gordon	the Parties
	Jethro Benton & Epaphroditus Benton	the Parties		John Gordon & William Powell	the Parties
	Isaac Benton & Robert Rale	the Parties		Francis Powell & Peter Brinkley	John Gordon & Demsey Jones
	Robert Rale & John Reed	one Party & Isaac Benton		Francis Powell & William Powell	John Slaving Demsey Jones
	Francis Powell & James Jones	one Party		Marm: Norfleet & Kader Ballard under Age	one Party
				David Jones & Moses Hare	the Parties

Carried over

(40)

Lines	Between whom	Who Present
	David Jones & Eliz.^a Norfleet	the Parties
	Moses Hare & Eliz.^a Norfleet	the Parties
	Bridget Wiggens & James Jones	the Parties
	Bridget Wiggens & Robt Peale	the Parties

Jacob Norfleet
his
David D I Jones
mark
Processioners

(41)

Oct. 23d 1764 Ordered that Isaac Hanel and David
Rice Do procession all the Lands from the Loosing Swamp
Down Perquimons Road to Speights Plantation thence by
the Cart Road that Leads to Elisha Hunters Then
Down by Meherin Swamp to Bennets Creek and
up the Creek to the Flat Branch then by the Loosing
Swamp to ~~the Flat Branch~~ perquimons Road
And make return thereof to April Court Next
According to Law Abraham Norfleet Clk vestry

(42)

For Mr David Rice
& Mr Isaac Hanel

North Carolinar Chowan County April ye 6th 1765 (43)
Possessioned Lines Between Elisha Hunter and John
Gorden Between Jacob Hunter and John Gorden Between
Jacob Hunter and James Jones Between Jacob Hunter and
Elizabeth Harrill Between James Jones and Moses Meazels
Between James Jones and Elizabeth Rice Between James
Jones and Isaac Spight Between Abraham Harrill and
Isaac Spight Between John Gorden and Thomas Fulenton
Between John Gorden and George Eason Between Isaac
Spight and Aaron Lauter Between David Rice and Samuell
Harrill Between Isaac Harrill and Samuell Harrill Between
Aaron Lauter and Samuell Harrill Between David Rice
and Elizabeth Harrill Between David Rice and Aaron Lauter
Between Aaron Lauter and Elizabeth Rice Between James
Jones and Elizabeth Rice Between James Jones and Abram
Harrill Between Aaron Lauter and Abraham Harrill
Between William Hinton and Abram Harrill Between Aaron
Lauter and William Hinton Between Aaron Lauter and Thos
Fulenton Between William Hinton and Thomas Fulenton
Between John Briggs and Thomas Fulenton Between
William Hinton and John Briggs Between Aaron Lauter
and Elizabeth Rice Between Isaac Harrill and Aaron
Lauter Between Isaac Harrill and David Rice Between
James Jones and John Jones Between Josiah Granbery and
John Jones Between Josiah Granbery and James Jones
Between James Jones and Elizabeth Rice Between Josiah
Granbery and Elizabeth Rice Between Samuell Harrill
and Elizabeth Rice Between Josiah Granbery and
Samuell Harrill ~ Carried over ~

Between Josiah Granbery and William Hinton Between Josiah Granbery and John Davis Between Josiah Granbery and Hugh Hill Between Josiah Granbery and Robert Powell Between Moses Spight and William Hinton Between William Hinton and James Felps Between Moses Spight and William Spight Between the Land Formerly belonging to Daniel Pugh and William Walles and Robert Laitter and William Bond and William Spight Between John Davis and Hugh Hill Between John Davis and John Briggs Between Thomas Small and John Briggs Between Thomas Small and Jesse Eason Between John Briggs and James Jones Tayler Between Luke Sumner and James Jones to Between Jesse Eason and Thomas Fulenton Between John Briggs and Luke Sumner Between Robert Powell and Francis Powell Between Robert Powell and Moses Spight Between Robert Powell and Hugh Hill Between Robert Powell and Luke Sumner Between the Land Formerly belonging to Daniel Pugh and Robert Powell and Moses Spight and Willis Jones and James Felps Between Willis Jones and James Felps Between William Spight and James Felps

Agreable to an order of Vestry Hereunto Enexed We the Subscribers have processioned all the Lines in our District From the Loosing Swamp Down Pequimons Road to Spights Plantation thence by the Cart Road that Leads to Mr Hintons Down Moherin Swamp to benets Creek up the Creek to the flat Branch then by the Loosing Swamp to pequimons Road

David Price
Isaac Harrill

Octr 23: 1764

Ordered that William Bond and Palatiah Walton Do pro=
=cession all the Land that are included From Meherin
Swamp Begining at Jacob Hunters mill up the Said Swamp
to the Piping Branch So along the Said Branch to the main road
and from the said road to Aaron Blanchard's Old Road and along
the Said Old Road to Bennets Creek road up the Said Road to
Bennets Creek Bridge and thence up Bennets Creek to the
Mill on Meherin Swamp and make Return thereof to
April Court Next according to Law

Abraham Norfleet Clk Vestry

(46)

January the 16th 1765 Were processioned all the Lines between Abel Martain and Esther Phelps

The Line between abel martain and Jemima martain

The Line between Demsey Clinton and Gabriel Laciter

The Line between William Hays and Gabriel Laciter

The Line between Gabriel Laciter and Maxeymillin minshaw

The Line betwen Gabriel Laciter and James Brown

The Line between Maxey minchaw and John Brown

The Line betwen James brown and Maxey minchaw

The Line betwen James brown and Jotham Laciter

James brown and Richard minchaw

The Line between James brown and Thomas Hoult

The Line betwen Thomas Holt and John Laciter

The line between John Laciter and mary alphin

The Line between Mary alphin and John Slavin

The Line between John Slavin and Aaron Blanshard

The Line between Aaron blanshard and William Bond

The Line between William Bond and micager Blanshard

The Line between micager blanshard and Timothy walton

The Line between Micager and aron blanshard

The Line between aron blanshard and Mary alphin

The Line between Aaron blanshard and Richard minchey

The Line between Richard minchey and Jotham Laciter

The Line between Aaron Senr and Aaron blanshard Junr

The Line between Richard minchey and Josiah blanshard
The Line between Josiah blanshard and Jotham Laciter —
The Line between Jotham Laciter and Gabriel Laciter —
The Line between Gabriel Laciter and Josiah blanshard
The Line between William bond and ~~George~~ Ozias Laciter —
The Line between George Laciter and Ozias Laciter
The Line between Ozias Laciter and Robert Laciter
The Line between Robert Laciter and abisha Laciter
The Line between Robert Laciter and Demsey Costen —
The Line between Demsey Costen and William Walton —
The Line between William Walton and Robert Laciter —
The Line between James Costen and william walton —
The Line between Richard bond and James Costen
The Line between James Costen and william Walton
The Line between William Walton and Richard bond
The Line between william walton william bond —
The Line between William Walton and Timothy walton —
The Line between Timothy walton and Micager Blanshard
The Line between William Walton and Palatiah walton
The Line between William Walton and Thomas Walton —
The Line between Palatiah Walton and Thomas walton —
The Line between Timothy walton and Robert Hill —
The Line between Robert Hill and Henry walton —
The Line between Henery walton and Palatiah walton —
The Line between moses Laciter and James Costen Refused to be Pro[illegible]
[illegible] moses Laciter —

(48)

In Obedience to an Order of Vestry Dated October the 23: 1764 We the Prossessioners hath Prossessioned all the Land from Meherin Swamp up the said Swamp to the Rping Branch So along the Sd Branch to the Main Road and Down the Sd Rod to Aron Blanshards old Road and along the Sd Old Road to Bennets Creek Road up the Sd Road to Bennets Creek Bridg and then up Bennets Creek to the Mill on Meharin Swamp

Pelatiah Walton

William Bond

(49)

Agreable To anorder of [illegible] here unto [illegible]
We The Subscribers have [illegible] all the Lines
In our Destricts Except one Line Betwen Thomas [illegible]
and James parker the [illegible] hoskens Neglect to Shew the Line
from The Indian Town Creek to Sandy [illegible] on [illegible]
Chowan River To the perquimon Road
as Witnes our hands — —

David Welch
William Copeland

In Obedience to an order of Vestry Dated october 23d: 1764 we the processioners have processioned the Lines hereunder mentioned Viz. (50)

Lines	Between Whom	Who present	Lines	Between Whom	Who present
	John Craven & Saml Swift	the parties		Daniel Earl & Peter Parker	the parties
	John Craven & Wm Harlow	the parties		Wm Boyd & Peter Parker	Peter Parker
	Saml Swift and Wm Harlow	the parties		Wm Boyd & Wm Bond	one party
	Saml Swift & Thos Hubbert	the parties		Wm Bond & John Baccus	the Parties
	Wm Harlow & Rebecca Gilbert	the parties		Wm Boyd & John Baccus	one party
	Wm Stewart & Rebecca Gilbert	the parties			
	Abm Norfleet & Rebecca Gilbert	the parties			
	Abm Norfleet & Wm Stewart	the parties			
	Wm Stewart & Saml Swift	one party and Phillip Meguire			
	Abm Norfleet & Saml Meguire	the parties			
	Miles Halsey & Saml Meguire	the parties			
	Miles Halsey & Prisilla Woodard under age	Miles Halsey			
	Saml Woodard & Richd Woodard under age	Ann Woodard			
	~~Saml Woodard & Wm Boyd~~				
	Saml Woodard & Richd Glohon	the parties			
	Wm Boyd & Richd Glohon	Richd Glohon			
	Wm Boyd & Thos Holliday	the parties			
	Luke White & Wm Boyd	Luke White			
	Daniel Earl & Luke White	the parties			

Peter Parker } Processioners

Samuel his mark Meguire

These Lines hereunder are unprocessioned for the Reasons as follows (51)

John Paget & } Craven Refusing
John Craven }

Thos Hubbert & } Swifts Refusing
Saml Swift }

Thos Hubbert & } Bunch Refusing
Jesse Bunch }

Sarah Lewis } Bounds uncertain
& Jesse Bunch }

Shadrach Bunch } neither of them appearing
& Sarah Lewis }

John Campbell } Campbell not in the Country
& Shadrach Bunch }

Wm Boyd and } Campbell not in the Country
John Campbell }

Wm Boyd & } B[illegible]
Saml [illegible] }

John Campbell } Campbell not in the Country
& Sarah Lewis }

(52)

North Carolina } ss — Aprile Inferior Court
Chowan County — } 1765 —

Present His Majesties Justices

It was then & there ordered that Elisha Hunter Esquire Surveyor of this County & William Bond, James Bond, Hance Hoffler & Abraham Norfleet go round the lines of Mr. William Boyd's Lands in this County between him & Samuell Woodward & that the said Freeholders be sworn according to Law & that Elisha Hunter Esqr. return the same to next Court.

Test Thos. Jones Clerk

(53)

Order to Procession
The lines between
Mr. Willm. Boyd
& Samuell Woodward

Mr. Boyd refusing

The Within Order Not Executed as it appeared to be a mistake in the Possessioners Return the Line Refused to be porsesioned Was beteen Mr. Wm. Boy & Richard Meglohan as S. Woodward haveing Sold the Sd Land to Meglohan

Elisha Hunter

In Obedience to an order of Vestry Dated october 23d. 1764
We the Processioners Have Processioned Lines following Vizt.

Lines	Between Whom	Who Present	Lines	Between Whom	Whom Present
	Joseph Rogers & Thos Hoskins Junr	Joseph Rogers		Charles Jordan Junr & John Jordan Junr	the Parties
	Joseph Rogers & Charles Roberts	the Parties		Charles Jordan Junr & Jacob Ellis	the Parties
	Thos Hoskins & Charles Roberts	Wm Roberts & Siles Robert		Charles Jordan & Evan Skinner	Charles Jordan
	Charles Roberts & John Parrish	the parties		Evan Skinner & Jacob Ellis	Jacob Ellis
	David Humphries & John Parish	the parties		Evan Skinner & Wm. Simsons	the Parties
	David Humphrys & Charles Roberts	the Parties		Wm Simson & Jacob Ellis	the Parties
	David Humphrys & Wm Halsey	the Parties		Jacob Ellis & John Brin	the Parties
	David Humphrys & Wm Ashley	David Humphrys		Jacob Ellis & Ephraim Ellet	the parties
	Wm Ashly & John Parrish	John Parish		John Jordan & John Brin	John Jordan
	Lewis Ward & Wm Ashley	Wm Ashley		John Brin Francis Smith	John Brin
	Lewis Ward & Wm Muns	Wm Muns		Hance Hofler & Francis Smith	Hance Hofler & James Harris
	Thos Muns & Wm Muns	the Parties		James Harris & Francis Smith	James Haris
	Thos Muns & Demsey Bond under age	Thos Muns		John Brin & John Simson	John Brin
	Saml Kid & Charles Jordan Junr	the Parties		John Brin & Ephraim Ellet	Ephraim Ellet
	Charles Jordan Junr & Wm Muns	Wm Muns			
	Charles Jordan Senr & Charles Jordan Junr	the Parties			
	Charles Jordan Senr & John Parish	John Parish			
	Charles Jordan Senr & John Jordan Junr	John Jordan			

(54)

The Lines Between the persons Hereunder Named are unprocessioned for the following Reasons

Thomas Hoskins Senr } Hoskins Refusing
Wm Bond

Thos Hoskins Senr } Hoskins Refusing
James Bond

Thos Hoskins Senr } Hoskins Refusing
Hances Hofler

Thos Hoskins } Hoskins Refusing
John Parish

Thos Hoskins Senr } Hoskins Refusing
Wm Halsey

Thos Hoskins Senr } Hoskings Refusing
Lewis Jordan

Thos Hoskins Senr } Hoskins Refusing
Wm Ashley

Patrick Hix } Hix Refusing
Wm. Cotteral

Joshua Deal } Deal Refusing
Mary Simson

Thos Streator } Streator Sick not able to appear
Charles Robert

Thos Luten Senr } Luton Not able to Go
Thos Mckider

Joseph Parrish
Thos his T Baccus mark

Processioners

North Carolina ss April Inferior Court 1765. (56)
Chowan County ss

Present His Majesties Justices

It was then and there ordered that Elisha Hunter Esquire Surveyor of this County and Messrs Evan Skinner, William Cotterell, Charles Jordan Senior, & Thomas McKidor do Proceed by the Lines running between Thomas Hoskins Senior and ~~John Curri~~ Guilliam Hatfy and that the said Freeholders be sworn According to Law and that Elisha Hunter Esquire return the Same to next Court.

Test Thos Jones Clerk

Order to Provision
between Thomas
Hopkins Senior &
Willm Halsey

Thomas Hopkins the
Party refusing

(58)

North Carolina }
Chowan County } In Obeadiance to Several Orders
Of the P Infearior Court of Sd ~~Coun~~
Ordering Messrs Evan Skinner Wm Cottrell ~~John~~
Charles Jordan & Thos Mc,rider to go on the Lines
between Thos Hoskins & Wm Halsey Which we
haveing Done in the following manner. begining
at a Gum Standing on the No Side of the Branch
known by Name of Spring Branch & on the West Side
Of a Small Branch that Issueth out of Sd branch
Runing then With Sd its Several Courses to John
Robersons Corner pine then on Robersons Line it
appearing to us to be the Devideing line between Sd Hoskins & Slender
Ashley to Lewis Jordans line then on the line between
~~Sd~~ Sd Hoskins and Sd Jordan on the Oald bounded
line of marked trees Which appeared to be the Devid
-ing Line of Sd Lands to his Corner - - -
Then on the lands between Sd Hoskins and
John Parish ~~by~~ a New line of marked trees ~~as~~
as No Oald ~~ones~~ was to be found agreed on by the par
-ties begining Near a Poeoson Caled the Woolf Den ~~to~~
and Runing through Sd Wolf Den No 80d West to a
~~Rd~~ Red Oak Standing in a flat Branch then along
Sd Branch by a line of marked trees So 60d W to the
the Center of Three large pines then So 40 W along Sd
Branch to John Watsons Line then on Sd Watsons line
No 50 d W to his Corner - - - - -
Then on the lines between Sd Hoskins and Hanel
Hoffler So 55 W 132 pole - - - - -
Then on the lines between Sd Hoskins & Wm
Bond begining at a marked White Oak Standing on
the So Side of Deep Run Runing then So 34 d W
40 pole to a Smal Red Oak then So 70 Et to a Corner
pine then by the Oald bounded line to a Small -
branch then up Sd Branch to a White Oak then on the pat

(59)

tent line to the Senter of five pines Standing in a branch that Issueth outt of Deep Run then Down Sd Run to the first Station the afore Sd lines att Ren-ewed July ye 9th 10th 12th 1765 the afore Sd Freeholders Was first Sworn according to Law — — — — —

July ye 17 1765 then Messrs William Bond James Bond Hance Hoffler & Abraham Norfleet went on the Lines between Wm Cottrel & Patrick Hicks and Renewed the Old lines Which appeard to us to be the Bounds between Sd Cottreel & Sd Hicks they being first Duly Sworn according to law — — —

July ye 11th 1765 Messrs Thos Hoskins John Hoskins John Parish & Thos Backers Went on the Lines between Mary Simson & Joshua Deal and Renewd the Old bounded lines as appeard to us to be the bounds between Sd Simson & Sd Deal they being first Sworn according to Law Certified pr

Elisha Hunter

Mr. Hunters return's concerning Procesioners Returns

Willm ~~Isaac~~ Herrick his will aprile 1762

576

North Carolina }ss
Chowan County }

To the Worshipfull Justices of Chowan ~~County~~ (61)
Inferior Court At the Petition of John
Lewis Junior. Humbly Sheweth that
your Petitioner was Appointed with
Josiah Small by the Vestry of the Parish
of Saint Pauls to Procession certain Lands
&c within the County aforesaid your
Petitioner what with the very wet
weather in the winter & his crop coming
on after Aprill Court Last had it not
in his Power to Comply with the said
order of ~~Court~~ Vestry & your Petitioner therefore
most humbly prays your worships
to grant him the Continuance of the
said order untill the next Inferior
Court in October as by that time he

(62)

will have complied with the said order
& your Petitioner in duty bound will
ever pray &c.

John Lewis Junior

July 22d 1765

John Lewis Junior
his Petition
as one of the
Processioners

(63)

(64)

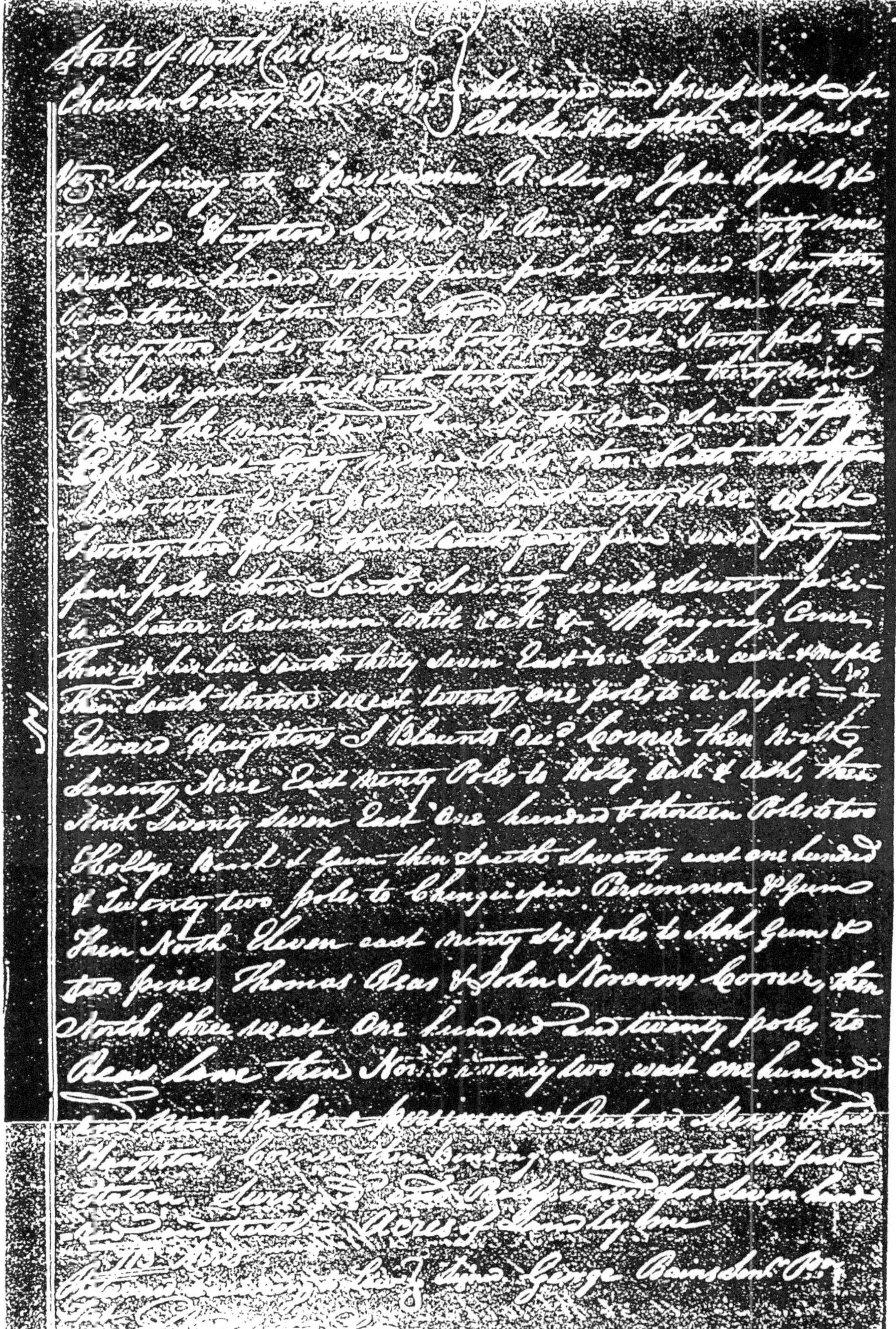

State of North Carolina }
Chowan County Dec 1795 } Surveyed and processioned for
Charles Haughton as follows

No 3 beginning at a Persimmon R. Merys Jesse Hassells &
the said Haughtons Corner & Running South sixty nine
West one hundred & fifty four poles to the said C Haughtons
[illegible] then up the said [illegible] North sixty one West
sixty two poles, then North forty four East Ninety poles to
a Black gum then North thirty three West thirty nine
poles to the [illegible] then up the Road South fifty
eight West sixty nine Poles then South thirty
West thirty eight poles then South sixty three West
Twenty two poles then South forty five West forty
four poles then South Seventy West Seventy four
to a Water Persimmon White Oak & McGregory's Corner
Then up his line South thirty seven East to a Corner ash & Maple
then South thirteen West twenty one poles to a Maple &
Edward Haughtons & Blounts decd Corner then North
Seventy Nine East Ninety Poles to Holly Oak & Ash, then
North Seventy seven East One hundred & thirteen Poles to two
Holly Beech & Gum then South Seventy east one hundred
& Twenty two poles to Chinquapin Persimmon & Gum
Then North Eleven east ninety six poles to Ash Gum &
two pines Thomas Rea & John Newcoms Corner, then
North three West One hundred and twenty poles to
Reas line then North twenty two west one hundred
and seven poles a persimmon Richard Merys & said
Haughtons Corner then binding on Merys to the first
station Surveyed and Processioned for seven hund
[illegible] Acres of Land by me
[illegible]
[illegible] George Barnes Sur

(2)

State of North Carolina }
Chowan County } September Term 1796 (65)

Surveyed for George Bains Senr William Bains Senr & George Bains the younger,

No. 3) this Plan represents the land in possession of George Bains Senr William Bains & George Bains the younger lying in Chowan County, Butted and Bounded as followeth, Beginning at a Cypress in Yeopim River Swamp Doctr Samuel Dickinsons line, & the County line, then running South 42½ Wt 246 poles Binding Thomas Wards patent line to a Bunch of Gums then Binding Trailors patent line So. 16 Et 48 poles to a water oak Jacob Blounts George Bains Senr & Thomas Wards Corner then with George Bains Senr Patent So 70 Wt 79 Poles to a gum & oaks then No 26 Wt 33 Chain to a poplar then So. 45 Wt 95 poles to Henderson Standins line thence with his No 64 Wt 208 poles to a white Oak then No 9 Wt 9 Poles to a pine Stump then No 29 Wt 47 poles to a pine by the Ponds, old field then with George Bains Senrs line No 17 Chains to a Gum then then No 60 Wt 52 chain to a pine & two Gums in Samuel Standins line by his fence then with his line No 5 Chain to two Sassafras then No 40 Wt 120 poles to a gum then Then No 49 Wt 96 pole to a pine Joshua Johnson & James Jones Corner then with Jones's line No 11 Wt 7 Poles to Michael [illegible] Corner water oaks, then with his line No 7½ Chain to a Gum & Maple then No 45 Et 58 Chain to a dead pine [illegible] Capt John Norcoms Corner tree, then with his line So 66 Et ~~38 Chain~~ to a pine in Eb Branchs line, then with his line So 18 Wt 20 Chain to a pine then So 5½ Chain to a Gum Ed Branchs, & Delight Nixons Corner tree then with Nixons line So 3½ Chain to William Lillyjohns line [illegible] then with his line No 78 Wt 32 Chain to a pine then South 36 Wt 10 Chain to a pine then So 7 Wt

102

(3)

13 Chain to a pine then So 59 Et 23 Chain to a pine on the South Edge of the Oak Land then So 85 Et 20½ Chain to a forked pine then So 68 Et 28 Chain to a pine then leaving Lilly's line So 14 Chain to a Green Oak Thomas Mings land Corner then with his line So 35 Et 17 Chain to a Cypress in the Aforesaid swamp then down the run of the swamp the Various Courses thereof to the first Station Containing 1675 Acres Surveyed June the 6th 7th 8th and September the 9th and 10th 1796

In Obedience to the Order of Court hereunto annexed I have processioned the Lines of the Lands of George Bains Senr. &c as above stated Present Jacob Blount Esqr. George Bains Senr. & Samuel Standin, When on their lines

Acres Land 1675 Signed Jo Reddick

Test J Worsley Clk

(66)

(67)

State of North Carolina } (4) Surveyed & processioned on the
Chowan County } 5th 6. 7th & 8th December 1796 & on the
16th & 23d of January 1797 for William Bennett
as follows. Viz. Begining at Rockahock Creek at
the side of the said Creek at Stephen Elliotts Corner and running
Along Elliotts line N. 89. E 170. poles to the path then S. 78. E
110 poles to a pine Hinsleys line Corner by the road then
along his line S. 50 E. 106 poles to a sweet gum his Corner
in Micajah Bunchs line then along Bunchs line N 32
E 85 poles to a popler & Gum, then S 34. E. 90 poles
to two white Oakes and a Gum then N. 30 E 65. poles to
a Center of 3 dogwoods and a pine Bunchs and Col.
John Bonds Corner Then along Bonds line N. 58. W.
120. poles to a Maple Then N 25. E 102 poles to a pine Then
N 41 W. 44 poles to a Black Gum Then N 55. E 65 poles to a
Sweet Gum in Bonds line Then N 55. W. 100 poles to a
White Oake Nicholas Newborns and Laurences Corner —
Then S 71. W. 60. poles to Newborns and John Coffields Corner
a pine by the Road Then along Coffields line N 69 W
124 poles to the Mill pond Then up the Mill pond to the
Mouth of a Branch near Parkers Landing, or the landing
By Parkers then up the said Reedy Branch the Various
Courses thereof to a poplar and Gum Then S. 40. W.
142 poles to an old Pine Ambrose Corner, now Nathanl.
Brengs Then along Breins and Abraham Norfleets line
N 38. W. 418. poles to 3 water Gums in the Juniper pocosin Then S. 47. W. 86 poles to two White Bays & a maple
and then William Lewis's line N 53½ W. 89 poles to
two pines and an Oak James Gorrons Corner Then
along his line S. 2½. E 275. poles to a pine a Corner
of John Pagett and Mrs. Mary McGuires Then
along Mrs. McGuires line S. 3. E 147 poles to a pine
Then S 74. W 355 poles to Chowan River Then Down the
River S 45. E 200 poles to Harrisons landing and still

(68)

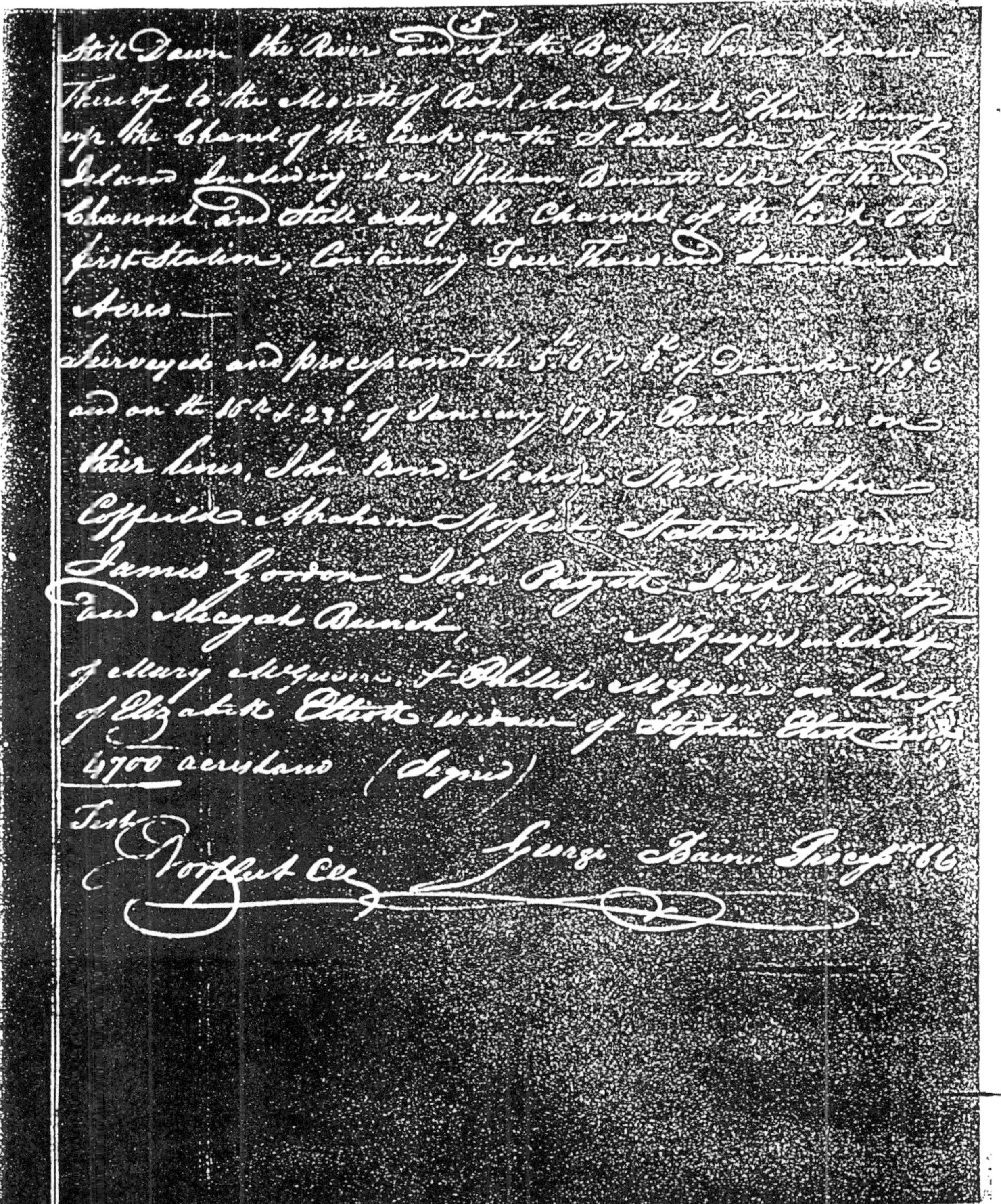

(5)

Still Down the River and up the Bay the Various Courses Thereof to the Mouth of Rockahock Creek, Thence Running up the Chanel of the Creek on the [illegible] Side of [illegible] Island Including it on William Bennetts Side of the said Channel and Still along the Channel of the Creek to the first Station, Containing Four Thousand and Seven hundred Acres —

Surveyed and processioned the 5th. 6. 7. 8th. of December 1796 and on the 16th & 23d of January 1797. Present when on their lines, John Bond. Nicholas Shelton, John Coffield. Abraham Norfleet. Nathaniel Brown. James Gordon John Pagett. Joseph Ainsley and Micajah Bunch, [illegible] McGuyer in behalf of Mary McGuire. & Phillip McGuire in behalf of Elizabeth Elliott widow of Stephen Elliott decd.

4700 acres land (Signed)

Test

[illegible] Norfleet Clk

George Baine Procsr. 66

(69)

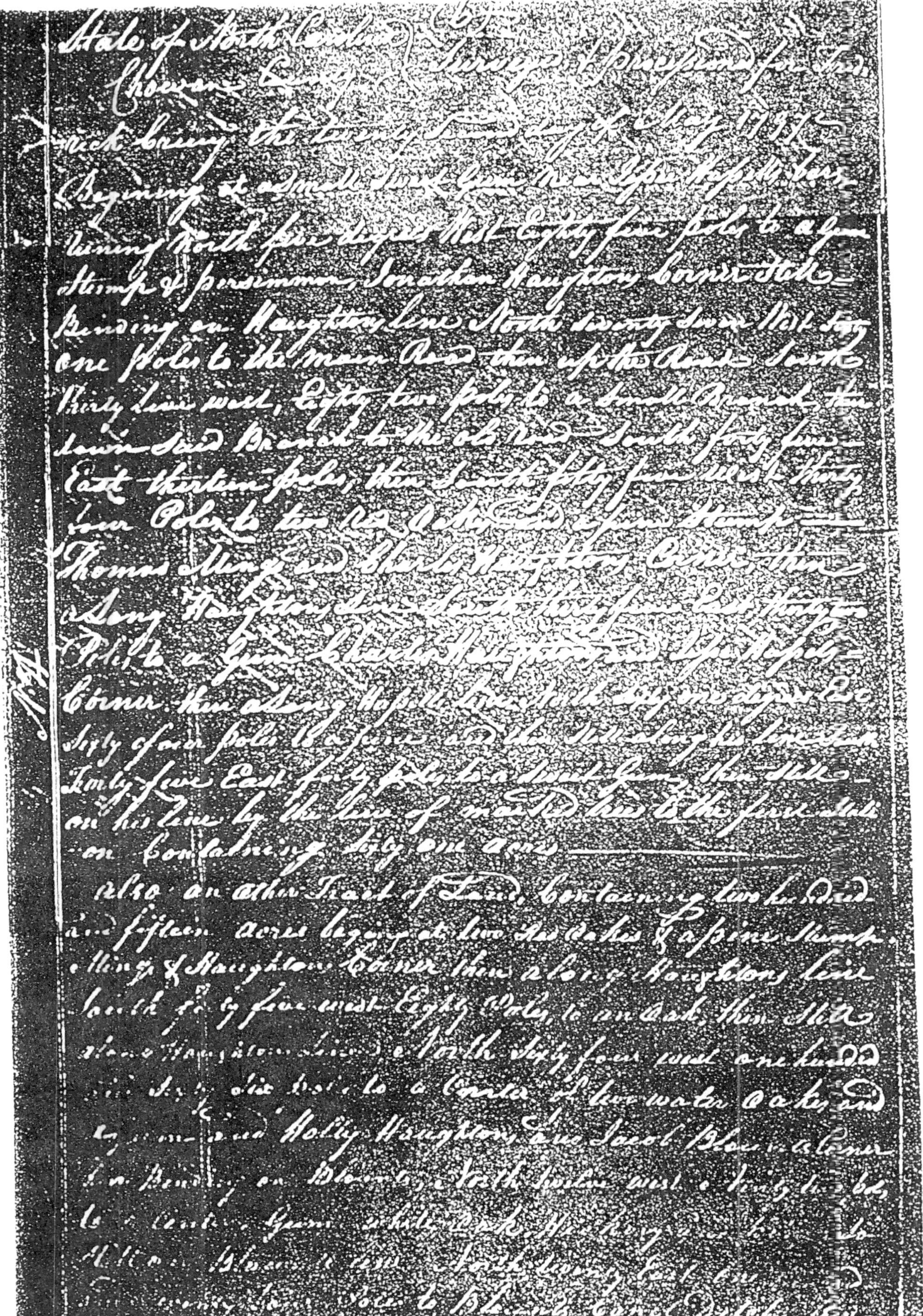

State of North Carolina } Surveyed & proportioned for [illegible]
Chowan County } [illegible]
[illegible] the twenty [illegible] day of May 1787

Beginning at a Small Sweet Gum [illegible] Hassells [illegible]
Running North five degrees West Eighty five poles to a gum
Stump & persimmon Jonathan Haughtons Corner Stake
Bending on Haughtons line North twenty seven West sixty
one poles to the main Road then up the Road South
thirty seven west, Eighty two poles to a Small Branch then
down said Branch to the old Road South forty five
East thirteen poles, then South fifty four West thirty
four Poles to two Red Oakes and a pine Stump
Thomas [illegible] and Charles Haughtons Corner then
along Haughtons line South sixty four East [illegible]
Poles to a Gum Charles Haughtons and [illegible] Hassells
Corner then along Hassells line North sixty one degrees East
sixty seven poles to a [illegible] then along his line South
twenty five East forty poles to a Sweet Gum then still
on his line by the line of marked trees to the first station
Containing sixty one acres

Also an other Tract of Land Containing two hundred
and fifteen acres beginning at two Red Oakes & a pine Stump
[illegible] & Haughtons Corner then along Haughtons line
South forty five west Eighty Poles to an Oak then still
along Haughtons line North sixty four west one hundred
and sixty six poles to a Corner of two water Oakes and
[illegible] and Holly Haughtons and Jacob Blounts Corner
then Bending on Blounts North twelve west [illegible]
to a [illegible] Gum white oak [illegible] Hickory [illegible]
[illegible] Blounts [illegible] North twenty [illegible]
[illegible] twenty five poles to Blounts Corner [illegible]

(7) (70)

Then Down said Ditch South twenty two East Seventy Eight Poles to a Center of two Gums and two Hollys on Allengs line then along Allengs line South Eighteen West one hundred and fifty eight poles into the Negro Plantation Then Still on Allengs line South fifty six East fifty one poles to a Dead Popler then South forty East Thirteen poles then South forty five East Eighteen Poles then Still on Allengs line by the Marked Trees to the first Station

61. acres (Signed) George Barns Processioner
215 of C. County
276 acres

Test Norfleet Ad

Present when on their lines, Jesse Hoyd, Jonathan Haughton Jacob Blounts Overseer Samuel Rea Delilah Alleng gave me her papers and Consented, Charles Haughton likewise give his Consent (Signed) George Barns P. C. C

(71)

State of North Carolina } (8)
Chowan County } Surveyed and processioned

for Mr. Edward McGuyer Woodward a Certain Tract or parcel of Land lying in Chowan County in the fork of Rockahalk Swamp where on the said Woodward now lives — Beginning at a Black Gum a corner of Julius Bunch, and John Coffield and Woodwards then binding on said Coffields line a cross the Ridge N 85 E 84 poles to a Cypress in a B. Branch a corner of said Coffields in Charles Johnsons line, then Binding on said Johnsons line along the run of said Branch to a Cypress in the swamp by the side of a ditch then down said Johnsons ditch to a Bridge, then Still down the run of the Swamp by Various Courses, binding on Bunches Land to the first Station Containing Sixty two Acres —

Surveyed & processioned the 8th day of November 1797. Present on their lines John Coffield, Charles Johnson & Solomon Bunch son of said Julius Bunch. 62 Acres

George Barns Surv. Pro.

Test J. Hoskins Clk

(72)

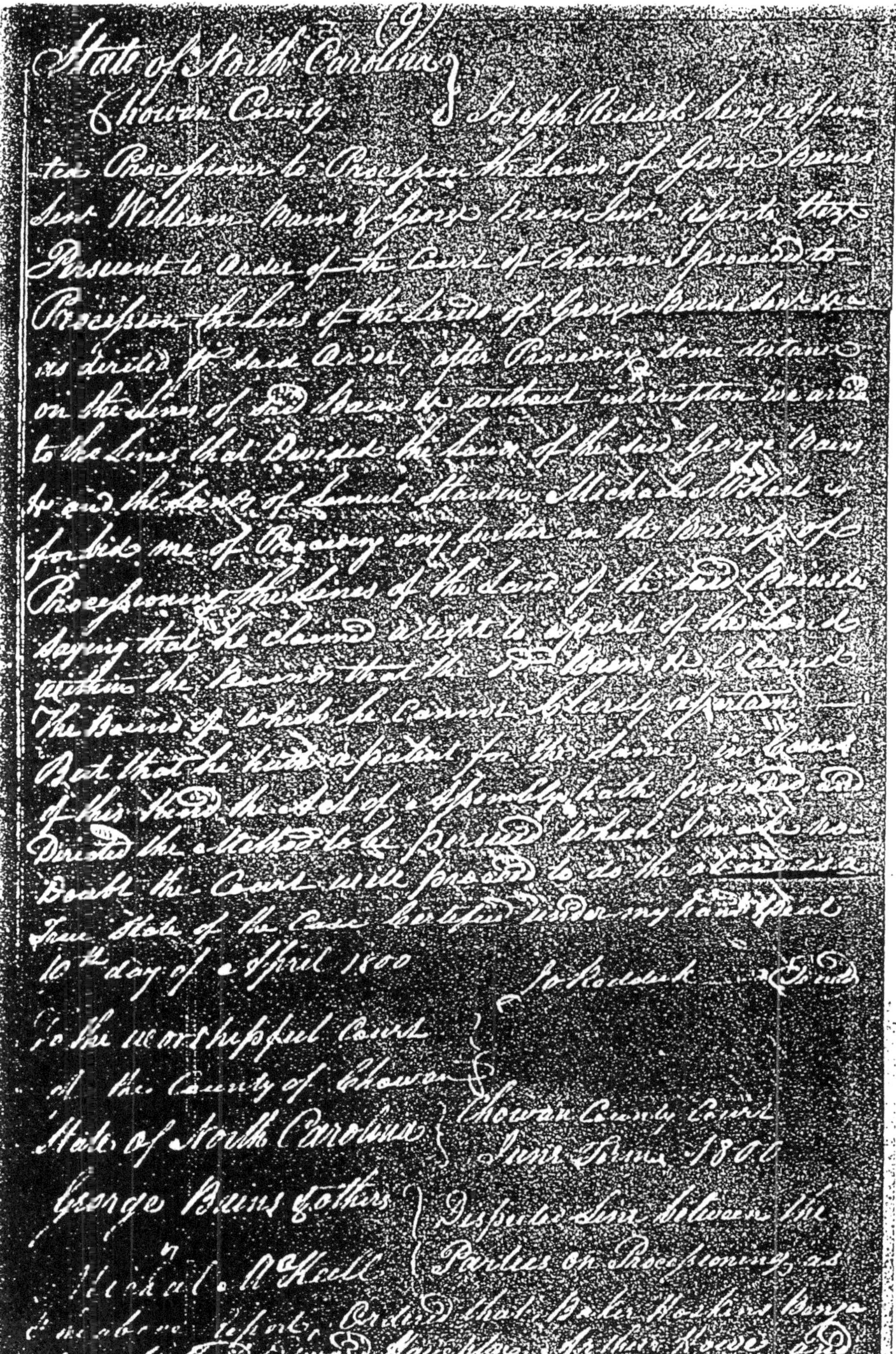

(9)

State of North Carolina }
Chowan County } Joseph Riddick being appointed Processioner to Procession the Lands of George Bains Senr. William Bains & George Bains Junr. Reports that Pursuent to Order of the Court of Chowan I proceeded to Procession the lines of the Lands of George Bains Senr &c as directed by said Order, after Proceeding some distance on the Lines of said Bains &c without interruption we arrived to the Lines that Devides the Land of the said George Bains &c and the Lands of Samuel Stanton Michael McHall forbid me of Proceeding any further on the Business of Processioning the Lines of the Land of the said Bains &c saying that he claimed a right to a part of the Land within the Bounds that the said Bains &c claimed The Bounds of which he cannot clearly ascertain — But that he hath a patent for the same, in cases of this kind the Act of Assembly hath provided and Directed the Method to be pursued which I make no Doubt the Court will proceed to do the above is a True State of the Case Certified under my hand & seal 10th day of April 1800

Jo Riddick (Seal)

To the Worshipful Court
of the County of Chowan

State of North Carolina } Chowan County Court
June Term 1800

George Bains & others
v
Michael McHall } Disputed Line between the Parties on Processioning as the above Reports, Ordered that Baker Hoskins Benja[illegible] Coffield Edward Humphries Arthur Howe and

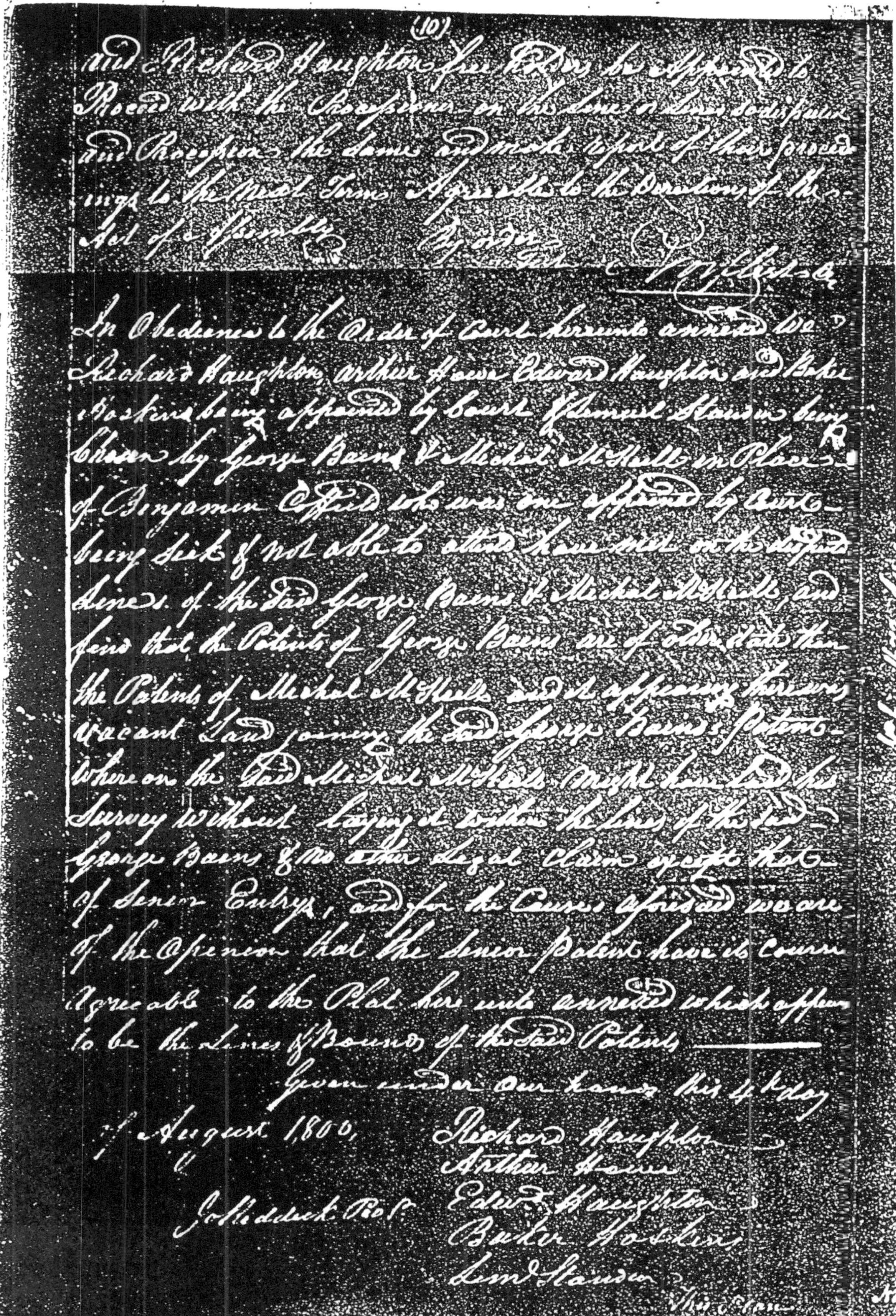

(10)

and Richard Haughton free holders be appointed to Proceed with the Processioner on the line or lines so disputed and Procession the same and make report of their proceedings to the next Term Agreeable to the Directions of the Act of Assembly

By order
Test [illegible] Clerk

In Obedience to the Order of Court hereunto annexed We Richard Haughton, Arthur Howe, Edward Haughton and Baker Hoskins being appointed by Court & Samuel Standin being Chosen by George Bains & Michal McHeall in Place of Benjamin Coffield who was one appointed by Court being Sick & not able to attend have met on the disputed Lines of the said George Bains & Michal McHeall, and find that the Patents of George Bains are of older date than the Patents of Michal McHeall and it appearing there was vacant Land joining the said George Bains Patent Whereon the said Michal McHeall might have laid his Survey without laying it within the lines of the said George Bains & no other Legal Claim except that of Senior Entry, and for the Causes aforesaid we are of the Openion that the Senior Patent have its Course Agreeable to the Plat here unto annexed which appears to be the Lines & Bounds of the said Patents ——

Given under our hands this 4th day of August 1800,

Richard Haughton
Arthur Howe
Edward Haughton
Baker Hoskins
Saml Standin

Jo Heddeck P.O.S.

(74)

(81)

This Plan Represents the Land in Possession of George Baines from William Baines & George Baines Junr lying in Bertie County — Beginning at a pine Stump on the Swamp of ... James Meys Corner thence So 42½ Wt 226 poles binding Thomas Warrs patent line to a Bunch of Gums then binding Trueloves patent line So 16 Et 58 pole to a water Oak Jacob Blounts and said George Baines Corner Tree then So 70 Wt 79 pole to a Gum & Ash No 16 Wt 35 Ch. to a poplar So 45 Wt 95 pole to Hendersons Standing line then with his line No 64 Wt 208 pole to a white Oak No 9 Wt 9 pole to a pine Stump No 27 Wt 47 pole to a pine by the Pond ... then with George Baines deceasd line No 17 Chains to a Gum No 80 Wt 52 Chains to a pine & two Gums in Lemuel Standings line by his Fence Then with his line No 5 Ch. to two Sassafrass, No 40 Wt 120 Poles to a Gum No 49 Wt 96 Poles to a pine Joshua Johnsons and James Jones Corner Tree, then with Jones line No 11 Wt 7 Pole to Michal McNeals Corner water Oak No 7½ Chains to a Gum & maple No 45 Et 58 Ch. to a dead pine Jos ... Capt. John Norcoms Corner Tree, then with his line So 88 ... 88 Chain to four Pines in Job Branchs line then with his line So 18 Wt 20 Ch. to a pine So 5¼ Ch. to a Gum Job Branchs and Delight Nickson Corner Tree then with Nicksons line So 32 Ch: to William Littlejohns Esqrs line then with his line No 78 Wt 32 Ch: to a pine So 36 Wt 10 Ch. to a pine, So 7 Wt 13 Ch. to a pine So 50 Et 23 Ch: to a pine on the South Edge of the Oak lane, So 85 Et 20½ Ch. to a forked pine, So 68 Et 28 Ch. to a pine then leaving Littlejohns line So 14 Ch: to a Gum & Oak Thomas Meys Corner Tree, then with his line So 35 Et 17 Ch. to a Cypress in the aforesaid ... River Swamp then down the Run of the said Swamp the various Courses thereof, untill it Comes opposite the first Station then to the first Station Containing Sixteen hundred & Seventy three Acres

No. 6 - 1673 Acres

The Line marked a b c d & e are the lines disputed by M. McNeal ... Geo. Baines

Jo ... Aug. 1800

(75)

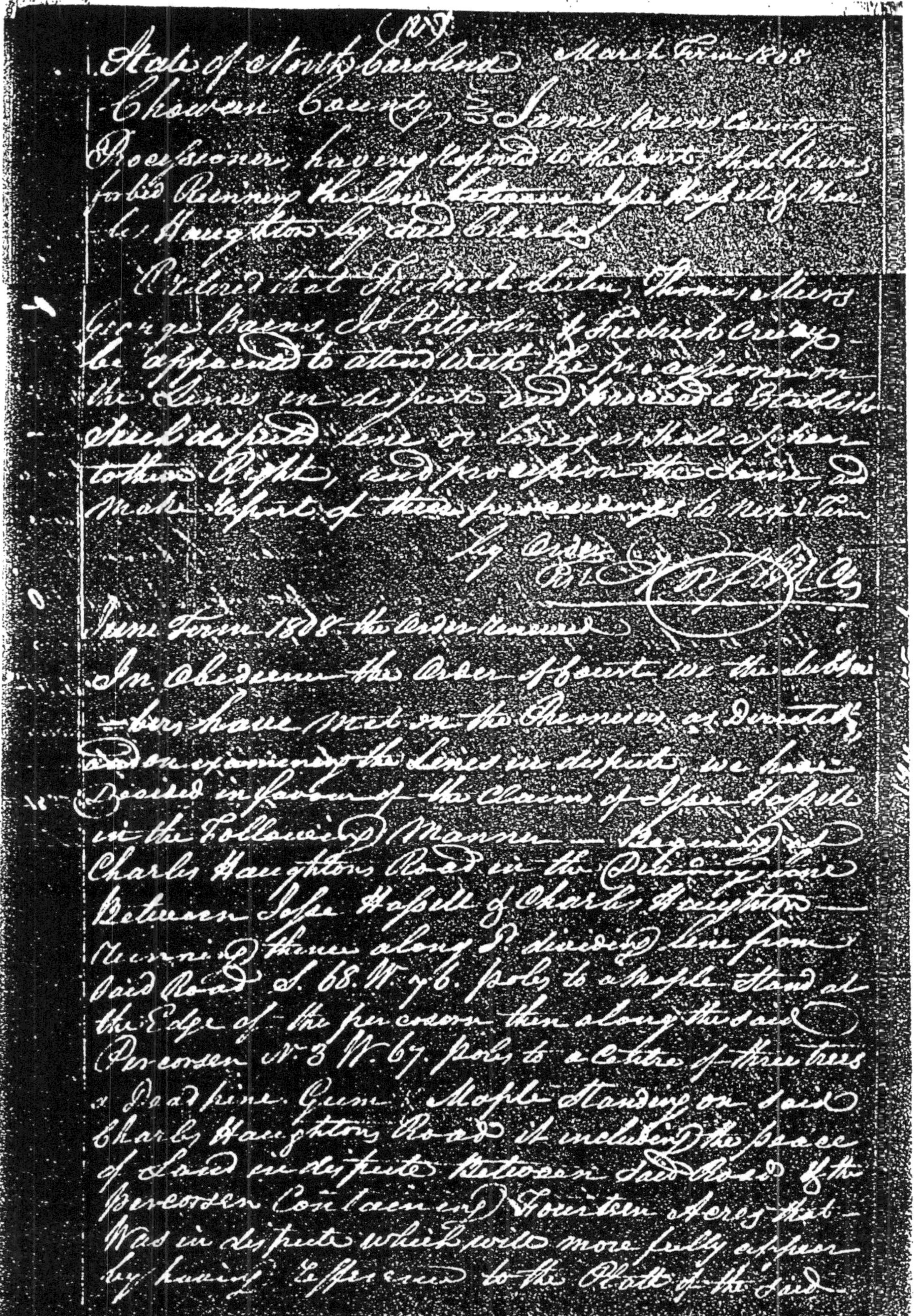

(No)

State of North Carolina March Term 1808

Chowan County } James Barns County Processioner, having Reported to this Court, that he was forbid Running the Line between Jesse Hassell & Charles Haughton by said Charles.

Ordered that Frederick Luten, Thomas Meers, George Barns, Job Pettyjohn & Frederick Creecy be appointed to attend with the processioner on the Lines in dispute and proceed to Establish Such disputed line or lines as shall appear to them Right, and procession the same and make Report of their proceedings to next Term

By Order
[illegible] Clk

June Term 1808 the Order Renewed

In Obedience the Order of Court We the Subscribers have met on the Premises as Directed and on examining the Lines in dispute we have Desided in favour of the Claims of Jesse Hassell in the Following Manner — Beginning at Charles Haughtons Road in the Dividing line Between Jesse Hassell & Charles Haughton Running thence along sd. dividing line from said Road S. 68. W. 76. poles to a Maple Stand at the Edge of the percoson then along the said Percosen N. 3 W. 67. poles to a Centre of three trees a Dead pine Gum & Maple Standing on said Charles Haughtons Road it including the peace of Land in dispute between said Road & the percosen Containing Fourteen Acres that was in dispute which will more fully appear by having Reference to the Platt of the said

78

Land that here with appears. Given under our hand this 7th day of Septembertr 1808

(76)

Job Patteyoton
[illegible]
Thomas Mirez
Fredrick Crerry
George Beash

The above Plott Represents a Tract of Land Surveyed and processioned for Tyse Hofsell. Begining at the Run of Creek Fork at the Foot of a Line Running up said Line S. 68 W. 232 poles to a Maple then N. 3 W. 67 Poles to a Centre of three trees Pine Gum & Maple then N. 45 E. 90 poles to Centre of 4 trees N. 55 E. 63 poles to Pine then S. 46 E. 41 poles to a Gum thence N. 64 E. 33 poles to a Gum N. 6 W. 47 poles to a Pine at the Corner of John Haughtons Land then N. 84 E. 84 poles to the Run of Creek Fork then up the Various Corses to an ash then S. 14 W. 21 Poles to an ash at the Run of said Creek Fork then up the various Corses of the same to the first Station it Being the foot of the Dividing Line Betwen Tyse Hofsell & Charles Haughton Surveyed and Plotted [illegible] 7th 1808.

155 Acres

James Beings C.S.

[illegible]
Mirez } Chain Barers

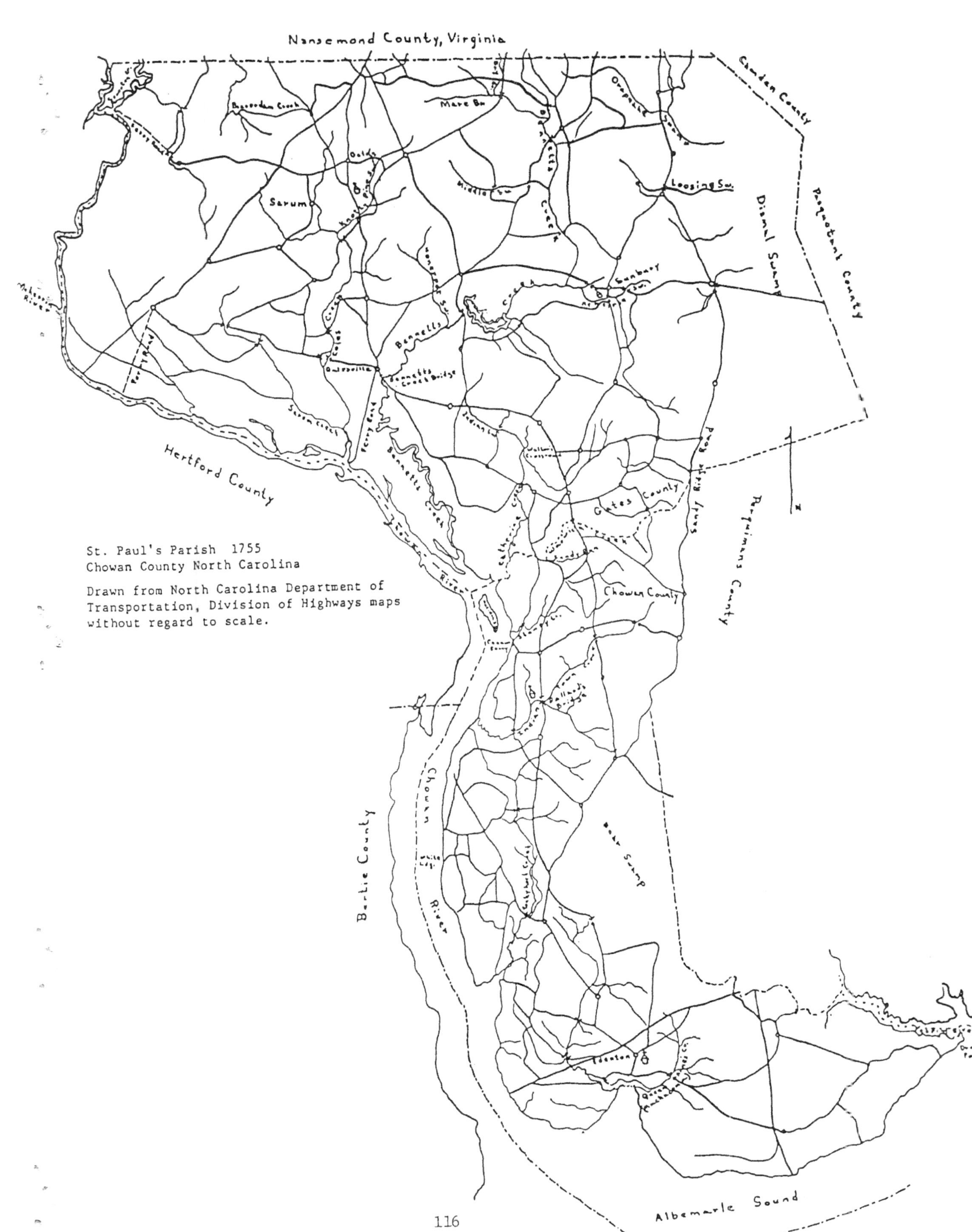

St. Paul's Parish 1755
Chowan County North Carolina

Drawn from North Carolina Department of Transportation, Division of Highways maps without regard to scale.

INDEX

INCOMPLETE NAMES

LOCATION INDEX

www.ingramcontent.com/pod-product-compliance
Lightning Source LLC
Chambersburg PA
CBHW051319020426
42333CB00031B/3410

* 9 7 8 1 6 3 9 1 4 2 4 9 1 *